# Be First Class

Insights, stories and tips to help you to be the best you can be personally and professionally

Stephen Pauley

# Be First Class

Copyright © 2016 by Stephen Pauley

The right of Stephen Pauley to be identified as the author of this work has been asserted by him in accordance with the Designs and Copyright Act 1988.

All rights reserved. This book or any portion thereof may not be reproduced or used in any manner whatsoever without the express written permission of the publisher except for the use of brief quotations in a book review or scholarly journal.

The content of this book is intended to inform, entertain and provoke your thinking. The author cannot be held responsible or liable for any loss or claim arising from the use or misuse of the content of this book.

First Printing: 2016

ISBN 978-1-5262-0197-3

Published by Be First Class Limited

www.befirstclass.co.uk

# Contents

|     | Introduction | 1 |
|---|---|---|
|     | Success – Ralph Waldo Emerson | 2 |
| 1.  | What untapped potential are you yet to discover? | 3 |
| 2.  | Create a clear personal vision for your life | 6 |
| 3.  | The power of visualisation | 9 |
| 4.  | Achieve your goals step by step | 12 |
| 5.  | Enjoy the present moment more often | 15 |
| 6.  | The purpose of life is simple….to be happy | 18 |
| 7.  | Great habits help you achieve your goals | 21 |
| 8.  | The value of self-discipline | 24 |
| 9.  | What clutter do you need to let go of? | 27 |
| 10. | Your beliefs drive your results | 30 |
| 11. | Set and achieve your personal goals | 33 |
| 12. | Keeping commitments | 37 |
| 13. | Mistakes can have positive outcomes | 40 |
| 14. | Be willing to be flexible | 43 |
| 15. | Every day is a gift | 46 |
| 16. | Lessons for effective teamwork from the Red Arrows | 49 |
| 17. | Don't wait for the right tools and circumstances | 52 |
| 18. | Persistence pays off | 55 |
| 19. | Play to your strengths | 59 |
| 20. | Watch your self-talk & keep it positive | 62 |

| | | |
|---|---|---|
| 21. | Practice gratitude and increase your happiness | 65 |
| 22. | Dealing with obstacles | 68 |
| 23. | Don't let adversity & setbacks hold you back | 71 |
| 24. | Put yourself first sometimes | 74 |
| 25. | Where are you investing your energy? | 77 |
| 26. | Always Be First Class – the A-Z for personal and professional success and fulfilment | 80 |
| 27. | Facing and overcoming fear | 82 |
| 28. | What would you like to attract into your life? | 85 |
| 29. | Never give up | 88 |
| 30. | Multi-tasking makes your brain smaller | 91 |
| 31. | Listening is the best form of influence | 94 |
| 32. | Maintaining a positive attitude | 97 |
| 33. | How productive are your meetings? | 100 |
| 34. | Negative experiences can have positive outcomes | 104 |
| 35. | Quality is a habit | 107 |
| 36. | Courage is a great quality | 110 |
| 37. | Taking time to express appreciation | 113 |
| 38. | Laughter is the best medicine | 116 |
| 39. | The importance of self-belief on results | 119 |
| 40. | Ask questions and avoid making assumptions | 122 |
| 41. | The power of random acts of kindness | 125 |
| 42. | Live now –procrastinate later! | 128 |
| 43. | You are never too old to pursue a dream | 131 |

| 44. | A different perspective on time management | 134 |
| 45. | Are you having fun at work? | 137 |
| 46. | Developing patience | 140 |
| 47. | What stops you asking for what you want? | 143 |
| 48. | Keep things simple – less is more sometimes | 146 |
| 49. | Turning a personal vision into reality | 149 |
| 50. | What's the worst thing that can happen? | 152 |
| 51. | We are powerful beyond measure | 155 |
| 52. | 16 Tips to help you to Be First Class professionally and personally | 159 |
|  | Promise yourself – Christian D Larson | 163 |
|  | About the author | 164 |

# Introduction

The main purpose of the book is to help you discover and fulfil more of your potential and to be the best that you can be.

The inspiration for the structure of the book came to me when I started publishing a weekly blog to the Be First Class website a couple of years ago. I've taken some of the most popular blog titles, adapted the content and added some new material. The chapters are a mixture of topics that affect personal and professional lives.

Modern life is busy, so I've written the book with short chapters in a style that will enable you to fit reading and reflection into a busy schedule. I've divided it into 52 chapters which contain insights, stories and tips. Each chapter also includes a thought provoking and inspiring quotation and questions to help you reflect and find the right answers for you.

It's your very own personal development programme. You can choose to focus on one chapter each week or at a slower or faster pace to suit you. Alternatively, you can read the book cover to cover and then go back to complete the various exercises and answer the questions. The choice is yours.

My wish is that by me sharing information and knowledge you glean an insight or take away a piece of information that has a positive impact on your life and results. Hopefully your insight will also make a positive difference to the lives of others. Your example could be a source of inspiration and encouragement to other people to be the best they can be. It can be like a positive ripple. I hope you enjoy reading the book.

Best wishes, Stephen.

encouraged to "be the best they can be" or had access to the right support to stretch and challenge themselves. Over the years I've found that when clients do take the time to focus on their needs and desires they find the process hugely rewarding. They get significant clarity and discover hidden gifts and treasures.

Although we may share some habits, beliefs and interests with other people, we're all unique and have the choice and chance to write our own life scripts. We all have the opportunity to reduce pressure on ourselves when we quit comparing our results in life to that of others.

Instead we can choose to review our progress against the goals and standards that we set for ourselves. I firmly believe that the right answers for our unique life experience rest inside all of us. However, to discover the right answers, occasionally we need to create some space to reflect and ask ourselves some key questions.

A great illustration of how answers can be close by and right under our nose is the following story that I came across many years ago which was told by Earl Nightingale. He was a great speaker and author and known as the "Dean of Personal Development."

Earl Nightingale talked about a farmer who lived in Africa and became tremendously motivated about looking for diamonds. An abundance of diamonds had already been discovered on the African continent. The farmer got so excited about the idea of finding millions of pounds worth of diamonds, that he sold his farm to head out to the diamond line. He wandered all over the continent. Years slipped by as he constantly searched for diamonds and wealth, which he never found. Eventually he went completely broke and threw himself into a river and sadly drowned.

Meanwhile, the new owner of the farm picked up an unusual looking rock about the size of a country egg and put it on his mantle as a sort of curiosity. A visitor stopped by and started exploring the rock on the farmer's mantle. The farmer was astounded to be told by the visitor that that the funny looking rock was about the biggest diamond that had ever been found.

The new owner of the farm said, 'the whole farm is covered with them' and sure enough it was. Prior to going off in his search for diamonds, the original farmer was literally standing on 'Acres of Diamonds' until he sold his farm.

Earl Nightingale said that each of us is right in the middle of our own 'Acre of Diamonds' if only we would realize it and develop the ground we are standing on before charging off in search of greener pastures.

**Reflection time:**

Pause for a few moments and reflect on the following questions:

What brings you the greatest happiness and satisfaction in life?

What personal accomplishments are you most proud of?

## 2. Create a clear personal vision for your life

**"Vision without action is merely a dream. Action without vision just passes the time. Vision with action can change the world." Joel A. Barker.**

I've discovered that the more time that people dedicate to deciding what they want to achieve in their personal and professional life and getting clarity on their personal vision, the more of their potential they discover and use.

It appears anything is possible when you have a clear vision and are in touch with your inner wisdom. When you truly believe that you can accomplish whatever you put your mind to, your dreams begin to become a reality.

However, it's very easy for the busyness of life, responsibilities, unimportant tasks and unhelpful habits to get in the way and stop us being the best that we can be. Life passes by really fast and our deepest held desires and dreams can get pushed to one side whilst we just cope with the demands of modern life and put the needs of others before our own sometimes.

I often get my coaching clients to create a vision poster made up of words and pictures using a poster size piece of card or flipchart paper which details their personal and professional vision. This helps them to get clarity on what they want from life and to provide a clear focus for personal action.

When creating the poster, the idea is that you focus on what you want and allow your creative sub conscious mind to wander through images and phrases in magazines, brochures, leaflets, newspapers or on-line. You can also use your own photographs or images from postcards. Essentially you visually represent anything that you want to attract into your life. The poster can cover a period that you are most comfortable with. It can be the next 12 months, 5 or 10 years or more. Everyone is different and there is no right or wrong period. The important factor is that you uncover your true desires and represent that in your vision.

If you would like to create your own vision poster, I suggest that you place a picture of yourself in the centre of it, so that there's a personal connection with what you create. The poster's content doesn't have to be completely new stuff. It can include things and activities that you're already involved in that you would like to sustain or develop further.

I recommend that you take some time to think about what you would like to Be, Do, Have in life and maybe jot down some thoughts in a notebook prior to starting to create the poster.

This is what I mean by Be, Do, Have:-

**Be** – the qualities and behaviours that you would like to use and display and what you would like to be known for.

**Do** – what you would like to do and experience in life?

**Have** – what you would like to acquire in life?

When doing this exercise consider all aspects of life - family, relationships, career, money, home, health and fitness, personal development, friends, hobbies, fun and recreation and if appropriate spirituality and volunteer work. There may be some specific results you wish to achieve.

Some examples I've seen people include on their posters include:- a fit healthy body, a loving relationship, financial freedom, starting a business, gaining promotion or qualifications, places to visit, acquiring material possessions, owning a house by the sea etc.

When contemplating what you'd like to include in your vision, the following questions may be useful for you to reflect upon:

- What are the strengths and character traits that you display in the various roles that you have to perform in life?
- What ambitions and dreams would you like to fulfil?
- What steps can you take to improve your health & fitness?
- What action will improve your financial position?
- What can you do to develop your relationships?
- What places would you like to visit?
- What skills would you like to develop/learn?
- What community projects would you like to be involved in?
- What hobbies do you enjoy or would like to pursue?
- What would you like to own or acquire?

Once your poster is complete, I suggest you place it on a wall at home or take a picture and put it on your phone, pc or tablet. Review it daily and consider what action steps you can take to make your vision a reality.

**Reflection time**

Pause for a few moments and reflect on the following question:-

What would you like to achieve professionally and personally over the next 12 months?

## 3. The power of visualisation

> "Whatever the mind can conceive and believe it can achieve." Napoleon Hill.

Once you have created a personal vision, you can start to visualise yourself achieving and experiencing the various goals that make up your vision.

Visualisation is the act of creating compelling and vivid pictures in your mind. It activates the creative powers of your sub conscious mind. It's a practice used by many people from all walks of life to help them accomplish their goals. Many sports people use the technique as part of their training and preparation.

There is a part of the brain known as the reticular activating system (RAS) that plays a vital part in your ability to achieve goals. Your RAS is the automatic mechanism inside your brain that brings relevant information to your attention.

The RAS will help you spot opportunities that will move you towards your vision. It acts as a kind of filtering system between your conscious and subconscious minds. It takes instructions from your conscious mind and passes them on to your subconscious.

It focuses your brain to notice available resources that were always present but had previously gone unnoticed. On your next journey try it for yourself by looking out for yellow cars. These cars would have been on your journey but you may not have noticed them if you hadn't made a point of consciously looking for them. You may be surprised by how many you spot!

Researchers have found that when you perform a task in life, your brain uses the same processes it would if you were merely visualising the task. Your brain sees no difference between visualising something and doing it. Your RAS can't distinguish between 'real events' and 'synthetic' reality. In other words it tends to believe whatever messages you give it.

Visualisation actually magnetizes and attracts to you, the people, resources and opportunities that you need to achieve a goal. If you give it images of your dream house, your perfect partner, the career that you would like or the places you want to visit, it will provide ideas and solutions to help you achieve those dreams.

My favourite visualisation story is the story about Major James Nesmeth, originally featured in the book Chicken Soup for the Soul by Jack Canfield and Mark Victor Hansen.

Major Nesmeth had a dream of improving his golf game and he developed a unique method of achieving his goal. Until he devised this method, he was just your average weekend golfer, shooting in the mid- to low- nineties. Then, for seven years, he completely quit the game; he never touched a club and didn't set foot on a golf course.

Ironically, it was during this seven-year break from the game that Major Nesmeth came up with his amazingly effective technique for improving his game – a technique we can all learn from. In fact, the first time he set foot on a golf course after his hiatus from the game, he shot an astonishing 74!

He had cut 20 strokes off his average without having swung a club in seven years and his physical condition had deteriorated.

Major Nesmeth's secret was visualisation as he spent those seven years as a prisoner of war in North Vietnam. During this time he was imprisoned in a cage approximately four and one-half feet high and five feet long.

For the majority of time he was imprisoned, he saw no one, talked to no one and experienced no physical activity. During the first few months he did virtually nothing except hope and say prayers for his release. Then he realised he had to find some way to occupy his mind or he would lose his sanity and probably his life. That's when he learned to visualise.

Every day, he played a full 18 holes of golf and he experienced everything to the last detail including seeing himself dressed in his golfing clothes, the smell of the trees and grass. He imagined different weather conditions covering spring, summer, autumn and winter. He also felt the grip of the club in his hand.

It took him just as long in an imaginary time to play 18 holes as it would have taken in reality. He did this seven days a week, four hours a day, eighteen holes for seven years. He took twenty strokes off his game and shot a 74.

**Reflection time**

Pause for a few moments and reflect on the following question:-

What resources, people, ideas or information would you like your RAS to spot to help you achieve your personal and professional vision?

## 4. Achieve your goals step by step

**"Step by step and the thing is done." Charles Atlas.**

Small and incremental steps applied consistently lead to outstanding results. Life is all about margins, there's often a tiny difference between winning and losing, perceived success and failure, hitting or missing a target. I'm sure you can think of examples from your own life experiences where the tiniest of margins determined the outcome of a situation.

We all sometimes mistakenly think that we have to keep taking massive action to get a result or make change happen in our life. The fact is that small incremental steps towards a goal accumulate into massive progress when applied consistently. One action per day applied every day of the year, towards a specific goal amounts to 365 separate actions. Achievement somehow seems bigger when you look at it like that!

As I am writing this, I am reminded of that famous African Proverb 'If you think you're too small to make a difference, try sleeping in a closed room with a mosquito'.

This quote reminds me to keep in mind the power of small! A small action is better than no action and nothing is achieved without some sort of action! The secret ingredient in success is action.

Recently, a client sought my advice about a fantastic vision he had for leaving his job and starting his own business. For some reason, despite him possessing the necessary skills, finance and having a great idea he was procrastinating. He wasn't taking sufficient action to turn the vision into reality.

We spent some time discussing what was behind this lack of activity and why things were stuck. There were a few reasons including not wanting to let go of the familiar or move out of his comfort zone and a fear of failure. However, the biggest obstacle was that the vision just seemed too big and overwhelming.

We agreed that small action steps applied consistently would be progress and help get things moving. I shared the story of "The Daffodil Principle" with the client as a source of inspiration and it helped him to get into action.

Every year, high in the San Bernardino mountain range of Southern California, five acres of beautiful daffodils burst into bloom. Amazingly, this special spot, known as "The Daffodil Garden," was planted by one person, Gene Bauer, one bulb at a time, beginning in 1958. This story originally appeared in Jaroldeen Edwards' book Celebration! The story contains details of a mother being taken to see the daffodils in bloom by her daughter Julie. Apparently, Gene Bauer's house (which was adjacent to the field of daffodils) had a poster on it which said:-

Answers to the questions I know that you are asking:-

- 50,000 bulbs
- One at a time
- By one woman
- 2 hands, 2 feet, and very little brain, began in 1958

Gene Bauer planted one bulb at a time to bring her vision of beauty and joy to an obscure mountain top. In doing so, she forever changed the world in which she lived. She had created something of magnificent beauty and inspiration. The life lessons her daffodil garden teach us are:

- Learn to move towards goals and desires one step at a time (often just one baby-step at a time)
- Ensure that we get pleasure from the doing
- Use the accumulation of time
- When we multiply tiny pieces of time with small increments of daily effort, we can accomplish magnificent things

After seeing the flowers in full bloom, the mother said to her daughter, "It makes me sad in a way, I'm thinking about what I might have accomplished if I'd thought of a wonderful goal thirty-five years ago. If I had worked away at it 'one bulb at a time' through all those years, just think what I might have been able to achieve!"

Her daughter summed up the message of the day in her direct way, "Start tomorrow, Mum," she said, "It's so pointless to think of the lost hours of our yesterdays. The way to make learning a lesson a celebration instead of a cause for regret is to only ask, how can I put this to use today?"

**Reflection time**

Pause for a few moments and reflect on the following questions:

Is there a task or project (professionally or personally) that you are procrastinating on?

What action step could you take to get things moving?

## 5. Enjoy the present moment more often

**"With the past, I have nothing to do; nor with the future. I live now." Ralph Waldo Emerson.**

October 21st 2015 was dubbed as back to the future day; as it was the date featured in the 1985 science fiction film "Back to the Future" starring Michael J Fox and Christopher Lloyd.

In the film, Marty Mcfly (Michael J Fox) meets up with his scientist friend Emmett "Doc" Brown (Christopher Lloyd) who unveils a time machine built from a modified De Lorean sports car and powered by plutonium from Libya. Its core component, a flux capacitor made time travel possible! Marty gets transported back to 1955 and he has to find a way back to 1985.

I remember seeing the film back in 1985 and I can recall thinking at the time that the 2015 date seemed a long way in the future and actually in another century! When I reflected on October 21 2015, it struck me that those 30 years have passed by so quickly.

Thirty years on from seeing the film, I thought this was the universe's way of giving a gentle reminder of the importance of really engaging with the present moment more often. What also occurred to me was that our brain has the ability just like the flux capacitor to travel through time.

It can transport us to the past and take us into the future. In doing so we may not fully engage with the present moment and all that it has to offer. This may mean that we are not fully present with the person or task right in front of us.

We can spend time thinking about what was, what could have been and projecting into the future, wondering about what may happen.

Modern life is demanding and it seems to have got busier. The world is changing at a faster rate than any other time in history due largely to the development of technology. We have access to more information, sources of entertainment and distraction than any other generation. We live in an information rich and time poor world.

It's easy to overthink things and not be present with what we are doing or where we are. When we have greater engagement with the present moment, we increase productivity and complete tasks in a state of flow. We listen more effectively and as a result have better connection and relationships with others.

Quieting our minds also helps us to feel centred, relaxed and have a greater sense of calm. This enables our mind to become clearer, giving us more clarity and increased focus. When we're in this state, life appears smoother, easy, effortless and things seem to flow more naturally.

Many clients tell me that they feel like they spend too much time locked in their heads and in doing so can feel overwhelmed and anxious. It's very easy to attempt to do lots of things and think about many issues all at once. Sometimes less is more. Many people have told me they perform better when they have less on their minds.

Our minds can quickly journey between topics like what to eat, the holiday we need to arrange, the meeting we've just attended or our next meeting. We can then flip to the number of unanswered e mails, how to solve a particular challenge or for those with children, focus on their schedules and logistics.

The more time we spend in our heads can lead us to feel less satisfied with life. By quieting our mind and focusing on the now, we can feel happier and in control.

Here are a few strategies to quieten the mind:-

- Work on focusing on one task at a time
- Set time limits for tasks and be assertive when it comes to interruptions
- Turn off email and social media notifications
- Dedicate specific times to check and deal with e mail
- If you do lots of work at a pc, take a 5 or 10 minute break regularly. Get up, stretch and walk around
- Use a breathing exercise to become more centred. Take a deep breath into the stomach to the count of 7; release it to a count of 7. Repeat this twice

**Reflection time:**

Pause for a few moments and reflect on the following question:

What action do you need to take to engage with the present moment more often?

## 6. The purpose of life is simple…to be happy

> **"Be happy with what you have and are, be generous with both and you won't have to hunt for happiness."**
> **William E. Gladstone.**

It was the Dalai Lama who said that the purpose of life is simple….to be happy. Happiness is a fuzzy concept and can mean different things to different people. There are a variety of factors that can have a positive impact on happiness levels and these can vary from person to person.

When I've asked clients what makes them happy, I've received many varied responses including success at work, seeing the family content, sporting triumph, listening to music, watching children enjoy themselves, time by the sea, reading a good book, going for a run, watching a film at the cinema etc.

As I've said we all have a unique definition of happiness, however there are some common characteristics and habits that I've noticed in happy people. They tend to:-

•Have a healthy balance between work and leisure time. They ensure they reserve and spend quality time with family, loved ones and friends.

•Possess an attitude of gratitude and freely express their appreciation for what they have and the good fortune they experience. They value and recognise the contribution of others.

•Do things for others and know that the world doesn't revolve around them. Acts of Kindness and generosity by them are common place and done without seeking credit or attention.

- Have a clear sense of direction and clarity about what they want to achieve and experience in life. They take the necessary steps to accomplish their goals.

- Work at developing collaborative relationships and avoid unnecessary conflict. They like to see people get along and work together in harmony. They don't have a need to be right all the time.

- Practice self-care and exercise regularly. They have healthy boundaries and identify when they need to put themselves and their needs first. They intuitively know when they need to rest.

- Be lifelong learners and accept that they never stop learning. They have a natural curiosity and aren't afraid to try out a new approach and step outside their comfort zone.

- Adopt a positive approach to life and have an optimistic rather than pessimistic approach to life. They see the positives in situations and look for the qualities in people.

- Be resilient and bounce back from adversity. They're aware that life has downs as well as ups and that challenges and difficulties are almost inevitable for a life well lived.

- Be comfortable with who they are and know that nobody is perfect. They have a strong sense of worth, understand their strengths and equally have an awareness of their weaknesses and flaws.

When I was training to be a coach we had to undertake practical sessions with our peers to develop our knowledge. During one of these sessions, I was asked what I'd like to achieve in life. My good habits. We truly are creatures of habit as research suggests that 90% of what we do each day is habit. Every day from the time you get up to the time that you retire to bed; there are hundreds of things that you do the same. This will include the way you shower, dress, eat breakfast, brush your teeth, drive to work etc.

The positive aspect of habits is that they free up your mind while your body is on automatic pilot. For example, you are able to plan your day whilst you are in the shower or driving to work. The negative aspect of habits is that they get locked into our sub-conscious mind and create self-defeating patterns that can inhibit our growth, limit our performance and prevent us from fulfilling our potential.

It was Einstein who said the definition of insanity is doing the same thing over and over again and expecting a different result. If you want a different set of results, you have to adopt a different approach. Your established habits are producing your current level of results.

If you'd like to create improved results, better relationships or greater happiness, it's important that you create good healthy habits that help you to maximise your opportunities and fulfil your potential.

Habits can hinder rather than help us and limit our results in life. These include overcommitting our time and spreading ourselves too thin, an inability to say no to unreasonable demands, not effectively managing distractions and interruptions, procrastinating and not following through on plans.

Some healthy habits that allow us to be the best we can be include:

- Creating a list of key priorities and plans each day
- Establishing a regular sleep pattern
- Returning calls and replying to e mails within 24 hours
- Spending time with positive people
- Exercising for 30 minutes and drinking 2 litres of water each day
- Limiting the amount of time that you watch TV
- Increasing the amount that you read and learn new things
- Keeping the promises that you make to yourself and others
- Being assertive and effectively managing interruptions.

Changing and creating habits takes time. As a result of comments made by Dr Maxwell Maltz in his book Psycho-Cybernetics published in 1960, it's been believed that it takes a minimum of 21 days to change a habit. However, research by University College London in 2010 stated that it may take as much as 66 days for a new habit to fully form. They suggest that the duration of habit formation is likely to differ depending on who you are and what you are trying to do.

**Reflection time**

Pause for a few moments and reflect on the following questions:

What new habits and behaviours do you need to start doing?

What good habits and behaviours do you need to expand?

What bad habits and behaviours do you need to stop doing?

## 8. The value of self-discipline

**"With self-discipline most anything is possible."
Theodore Roosevelt.**

In the previous chapter I talked about how great habits enable us to achieve our goals. A healthy helpful habit and personal quality I believe is vital in enabling us to achieve a goal, develop new habits or manage transition is self- discipline.

The dictionary defines self-discipline as "the ability you have to control and motivate yourself, to stay on track and do what is right." An example of how it can help with a goal like how to get fitter is ensuring you stick to a plan to get up earlier each morning to exercise no matter what the weather conditions.

It's controlling your actions, behaviours, habits, desires and the plans that you set for yourself. Quite often it's connected to self-development. Sometimes to achieve what you intend can mean doing things that you committed to even when you don't want to do them.

It's essential when you're looking to achieve a goal, start something new or develop a new habit that you get clear on why you want to do it and gain clarity on your motivation. Having a real understanding of your motivation will prove valuable if you encounter some difficulty, obstacles or some form of adversity when pursuing your goal.

Having this clarity means you can remind yourself why you're doing it and need to persevere if the going gets tough.

Self-discipline isn't about being hard on yourself. However, it is about being clear on what action you are going to take, being totally committed to that course and sticking to what is right for you. It's displaying inner strength, power and resolve when you encounter opposition and challenge.

Having great self-discipline helps develop self-esteem and confidence because you stick to your plan and stay true to yourself. This creates a positive spiral of good feelings, belief and attitude. It means that you fulfil your promises and commitments to yourself and others.

This helps strengthen relationships as you're seen by others as consistent, solid and reliable. You also build resilience and staying power which develops your ability to not give up despite setbacks or failure. It also enables you to resist distractions or temptation and deal effectively with obstacles.

A further benefit is that you can break down a large goal into bite size chunks which helps with feelings of overwhelm and to conquer procrastination or inactivity. You become more productive and efficient which means you increase the amount that you accomplish. You unlock more of your potential as you don't let fear, laziness or a lack of confidence get in the way of your progress and development in life.

There are a variety of ways that you can develop greater self-discipline. Prior to doing so, it's worth remembering the wisdom contained in the Chinese proverb "A journey of a thousand miles must begin with a single step."

**With this in mind:-**

**Start exercising your self-discipline muscle**

In order to build momentum I suggest you start with a small goal and micro actions. No change or development of a habit happens overnight. It requires persistence and commitment, so cut yourself some slack and be patient.

**Be honest with yourself**

Take some time to reflect and do some self-analysis. Have a think about what a lack of self-discipline is costing you and stopping you from accomplishing in life.

**Get clarity on your priorities**

Make a list of some goals that you would like to achieve or some behaviours/habits that you would like to change. Prioritise what's most important to you and concentrate on that area first.

**Plan some action steps**

As I mentioned in chapter four, small steps applied consistently lead to outstanding results. Decide on some action steps and commit to action. The fortune is always in the follow up.

**Reflection time**

Pause for a few moments and reflect on the following questions:

Is there a goal or area of your life where you need to be more self-disciplined? If so, what action will you take to achieve this? What will be your first step?

## 9. What clutter do you need to let go of?

> **"Simplicity is the ultimate sophistication."**
> **Leonardo Da Vinci.**

In spring each year, many of my contacts like to declutter their home and work environments. It's a great opportunity to simplify and let go of things and create space for growth, new adventures and projects. Somehow the exercise combined with brighter weather and greater daylight seems to help people to feel lighter, clearer and more organised. It helps to sharpen focus and increases creativity. Many people find it easier to work in a clutter free environment.

The Oxford Dictionary defines clutter as a "crowded and untidy collection of things." Feng Shui expert Karen Kingston says that's only part of it and just describes clutter on a physical level. She says a more complete definition would be "things that you no longer need, want or love; items that are untidy and disorganized or too many things in a small space; or anything unfinished." I would add an overloaded busy mind with many priorities and incomplete matters which can be projects or emotions.

As well as creating space, letting go of historic papers, magazines, books and things no longer needed helps create greater clarity and freshens up our environments. Having clutter can affect our energy levels and make us feel tired, lethargic and maybe stressed. It can steal valuable time when we have to constantly search for things and mean we feel disorganized and frustrated.

Clutter can weigh us down, create a heavy feeling, keep us stuck in the past and mean we procrastinate. When all available space is taken up, there is no room for anything new to come into our lives!

In addition to physical clutter, we can have too much on our minds resulting in mental clutter. During coaching programmes, I regularly encourage clients to declutter their mind and simplify their thinking. I call this process "moving from clutter to clarity."

There isn't an exclusive list of what clients choose to let go of in this exercise but there are some common things that they choose to release. These include procrastination, over thinking and analysing issues, pleasing others and putting other's needs before their own, comparing their status and results in life to others, self-criticism. Completing this exercise leaves clients feeling lighter, brighter and more energised.

Having physical, mental and emotional clutter can prevent us from focusing on our key priorities, the people closest to us and what's really important to us. Everything we have has a call on our attention and the more clutter the greater energy that's tied up in mundane matters. When we clear out the clutter, it allows us to focus and put the valuable things in our life into perspective. It stops us being bogged down in the details of day to day maintenance.

The process of clearing clutter is all about learning to let go of the belongings and the feelings and fear that keep us holding onto an excess of stuff. Life's constantly changing, so when something comes into your life, enjoy it, use it well and when it's time, be prepared to let it go so you can experience new things.

When decluttering, after filing or boxing up things that are to be kept and stored, you may find it useful to put the physical clutter into various boxes/piles as follows:-

- Things to be thrown away or sent for recycling
- Paperwork to be shredded
- Items to give to others or charity
- Possessions to be sold
- Articles that need to be repaired

Sometimes we hold onto stuff because we are afraid to let go and don't want to face the emotions we may experience from sorting through it. It could be we're afraid of making a mistake and don't want to later regret getting rid of something. Fear suppresses positive energy and prevents us from you being who we truly are. However the rewards from having a good clear out are well worth it. Releasing clutter helps us to connect to a new vitality.

**Reflection time**

Pause for a few moments and reflect on the following questions:

Are there any things that you no longer use, need, want or love that you need to let go of?

What benefits would it bring you if you were to do so?

**10. Your beliefs drive your results**

**"If you think you can or you think you can't, you are probably right." Henry Ford.**

Our beliefs play a pivotal role in the results that we achieve in life and help to shape and influence our behaviour. Whatever we believe dictates how we respond to situations and determines how we relate to the people that we meet and interact with.

If you believe that you will achieve a goal no matter what life throws at you, then you are more likely to do just that, rather than someone who believes they can never have what they really want.

When a hypnotist hypnotizes someone, they insert a belief into their mind and this influences how that person thinks and behaves. During hypnosis a person can adopt a belief that an orange is an apple or that a pencil is far too heavy to lift. These inserted beliefs change the person's reality and what they believe they can and can't do. In much the same way we can all be hypnotized throughout our lives by the ideas we take on from others and believe to be true.

Most of our beliefs about ourselves and how the world operates are formed in early childhood. They are shaped by our parents, grandparents, relatives, teachers, past experiences, media, culture, peers, friends & religion. Aside from physical differences, it's our different experiences and beliefs that make us all unique.

We may have false beliefs that stunt our growth. An example of a false belief that was universally accepted was that the earth was flat and that if you sailed far enough you would fall off the edge of the earth. Often we don't realise what our beliefs consist of or how they have been formed but they influence every moment of every day.

Every belief has a structure to it which we can change if we choose to. It's like carrying a recording in our heads. If the recording is working for us, we can keep it and maybe update it occasionally. However, if the recording is limiting us, we can take it out and re-record it, so we have one that is working for us.

We accept opinions from influential people in our lives and hold them as facts. However, they aren't facts but perceptions formed through our experience and other people's views. Beliefs are views about us, others and the world. These views determine the decisions we take and the way we behave. If we want to change our results in life then the process starts with changing our beliefs.

Beliefs determine how we think and how we talk to ourselves (our self talk) and this determines how we behave. If we're overly self- critical or hard on ourselves then we won't necessarily enjoy the journey towards a particular goal. We'll feel stressed, anxious and frustrated from time to time. However, if our self talk is kinder, more encouraging and positive then the journey will be a more enjoyable one. We'll feel better and therefore behave more confidently. Our results are more likely to be more positive.

There are two types of belief. We can have empowering ones which help us to believe that we can achieve. They propel us forward towards our goals and help us to feel confident and good about ourselves. Alternatively, we can have limiting beliefs. These hold us back, hinder our progress and negatively impact our confidence levels. They mean we get in our own way.

In 1954, Roger Bannister helped to change conventional wisdom and beliefs that people held by breaking the four minute mile record. Prior to the race and his attempt to smash this barrier people had urged him not to try it. They'd told him it was dangerous and life threatening. However, he ignored all this advice and successfully broke the record.

Once he'd achieved this, four runners broke the record within a year because they knew it was possible and could be done. Following Bannister's achievement, athletes changed their beliefs. They told themselves they could do it and as a result their bodies performed more effectively.

There are countless examples of beliefs missing the point. Many said photocopiers, telephones and computers would not catch on. Look how those beliefs turned out!

It's important that we continue to challenge the beliefs we have and ensure they are working positively for us. All of us have the power and control over our beliefs which shape our self talk/thoughts, behaviour and ultimately our results in life.

**Reflection time:**

Pause for a few moments and reflect on the following questions:

What beliefs that you hold empower you and which limit your performance?

Is there anything that you're motivated to change?

## 11. Set and achieve your personal goals

**"Desire is the key to motivation, but it's the determination and commitment to unrelenting pursuit of your goal - a commitment to excellence - that will enable you to attain the success you seek." Mario Andretti.**

I've found that many people have goals and targets related to their jobs or business but don't always have goals related to their personal life. I'm a big advocate of personal goal setting and the merits have been validated by lots of people I've worked with who have successfully set and achieved their personal goals.

Setting personal goals ensures that time and energy is focused on what really matters. It enables people to fulfil more of their potential, to grow, develop and experience new things. It provides balance to life and a sense of accomplishment.

Goals don't have to be massive. They can relate to fitness and health, hobbies, personal development or leisure such as places to visit, concerts to attend or days out to be arranged. It's easy to overlook these things in the busyness of modern day life if we don't plan.

**Here are a few goal setting tips:**

**Be specific about what you want to achieve**

What would you specifically like to achieve and by when? For instance "to lose weight" is a goal. However a better goal would be "to lose one stone in weight by June 30th this year."

**Get clarity on your why**

Determine what's driving and motivating you to want to achieve the goal and why it's important to you. Getting clear on your motivations upfront helps you to maintain focus and remind you why you must persevere when you feel like quitting.

**Get clear on your current position**

It helps to have an honest and objective assessment of your starting position and consider any action you have already taken or personal experience you can call upon. This helps you to quantify how realistic the goal is and what needs to be done.

**Clarify any obstacles you need to overcome**

Obstacles may be personal limitations or limiting beliefs or external factors such as a lack of time, money, knowledge or skills. By clarifying what needs to be overcome helps you to start to think about ideas and solutions.

**Determine what support and resources you need**

Do you need some help or support? What personal strengths, people or resources will help you to accomplish your goal? Would you find it helpful to be accountable to someone? Sharing our goals with others can establish an accountability mechanism. An accountability partner can check in on progress and provide encouragement or challenge if required.

**Commit to action steps**

Establish clear action steps which you are 100% committed to. You may find it useful to break large goals down into smaller chunks. This helps to prevent a big goal feeling overwhelming. Being in a state of overwhelm can lead to procrastination and stop us from making a start.

**How will you celebrate?**

Determine at the start how you will celebrate and reward yourself when you achieve your goal. This provides added incentive and keeps you focused and motivated. It's easy to fall into the trap of thinking about what we haven't achieved and not take any time to celebrate and reward ourselves when we complete something.

**The following story contains my final tip**

There was once a bunch of tiny frogs, who arranged a running competition. The goal was to reach the top of a very high tower. A big crowd gathered around the tower to see the race and cheer on the contestants. The race began.

No one in the crowd really believed that the tiny frogs would reach the top of the tower. They shouted, "Oh, way too difficult! They will NEVER make it to the top" and "Not a chance. The tower is too high."

The tiny frogs began collapsing, one by one except for those who, in a fresh tempo, were climbing higher and higher….

The crowd continued to yell, "It's too difficult! No one will make it!"

More tiny frogs got tired and gave up… But one continued higher and higher. This one wouldn't give up! And he reached the top.

Everyone wanted to know how this one frog managed such a great feat. What was his secret? This little frog was deaf!

So my final tip is to ignore the pessimism of others who say that you can't achieve your goals and dreams. Listening to them can take your dreams from you. Stay positive.

**Reflection time:**

Pause for a few moments and reflect on the following question:

What will enable you to get better at setting and achieving personal goals?

## 12. Keeping commitments

"Keep your THOUGHTS positive because your thoughts become your WORDS

Keep your WORDS positive because your words become your BEHAVIOUR

Keep your BEHAVIOUR positive because your behaviour becomes your HABITS

Keep your HABITS positive because your habits become your VALUES

Keep your VALUES positive because they become your DESTINY." Mathatma Gandhi.

Much is written about integrity and its importance in developing trust and healthy relationships. It's a personal quality of fairness and doing the right thing in a reliable way. Being true to your word and honouring commitments made is also a major part of integrity. A story that illustrates how integrity can be easily developed relates to Mathatma Gandhi.

In 1931, Gandhi travelled to Britain to attend the round table conference and influence the British public over the plight of India under British rule. Here was a man with no perceived power. He appeared frail, dressed in simple robes with no political office and no wealth. He spoke for nearly two hours without notes and he mesmerized many members of parliament and the press. Since it was difficult for the press to reach Gandhi due to the crowds and security, the press approached his secretary, Mahadev Desai to ask some questions.

One of the questions they asked was how he was able to speak so powerfully for 2 hours without any notes! He said, "You don't understand. You don't understand Gandhi. You see what he thinks is what he feels. What he feels is what he says and what he says is what he does. What Gandhi thinks, what he feels, what he says and what he does are all the same. He doesn't need notes. You and I think things that sometimes may be different than what we feel. What we say depends on who's listening. What we do depends on who's watching. It isn't so with him. He needs no notes."

Keeping promises made to others is important but so is honouring the promises made to ourselves as these can often be overlooked. It's very easy to fall into the trap of meeting other people's needs and putting our own needs on the back burner. Placing insufficient value on our needs in this way can have a negative impact on self-esteem and erode inner peace. It's a reason why some people have inner conflict and don't achieve the goals they set.

Occasionally, it's useful to remind ourselves we have a choice before we make commitments and that there's only limited time available each day. Prior to making a commitment get into the habit of ensuring it's a good use of your time and something that you really want to do.

Also convince yourself you aren't just agreeing to do something to avoid conflict. This habit can be overcome by learning to say no more often, giving a greater priority to your own needs and being more assertive.

Many people apply a "no exceptions rule" to their personal commitments. Once they have decided what they're going to do, it's a done deal and non-negotiable. They no longer have an inner debate. Instead they focus on taking the actions determined by their commitment. It makes life simpler and frees up lots of energy that would be used up debating the topic internally. It's about being true to yourself and aligning your thoughts, feelings and actions in the way that Gandhi showed us all those years ago.

To conclude this chapter, I would like to share a great quote by WH Murray, a Scottish Mountaineer and writer.

*"Until one is committed, there is hesitancy, the chance to draw back, always ineffectiveness concerning all acts of initiative and creation. There is one elementary truth, the ignorance of which kills countless ideas and splendid plans; that the moment one definitely commits oneself, then providence moves too. All sorts of things occur to help one that would never otherwise have occurred. A whole stream of events issues from the decision raising in one's favor all manner of unforeseen events, meetings and material assistance which no one could have dreamed would have come their way.*

*I have learned a deep respect for one of Goethe's couplets: "Whatever you can do or dream you can, begin it. Boldness has genius, power and magic in it. Begin it now!"*

**Reflection time:**

Pause for a few moments and reflect on the following questions:

What action do you need to take to honour commitments you have made to yourself previously?

What existing commitments that you have need some form of renegotiation or amendment?

## 13. Mistakes can have positive outcomes

> **"Anyone who has never made a mistake has never tried anything new." Albert Einstein.**

Recently I was watching a football match and the referee made a very obvious mistake with a decision that he made. A player handled the ball deliberately to prevent a goal being scored by the opposing team. The rules of the game indicate that this is an offence which necessitates a player being sent from the field of play for the rest of the game.

Unfortunately in the heat of the moment the referee confused the identity of the culprit and sent the wrong player off the pitch. It caused a big fuss in the media and there were calls for the referee to be removed from the panel of elite referees for a period. The referee was said to be devastated by his mistake. The incident reminded me of a story I read about Alfred Nobel and how a mistake changed the destiny of his life.

Alfred Nobel was born in Sweden in 1833 and was a chemist, engineer, innovator and armaments manufacturer. He was one of the most successful entrepreneurs of the nineteenth century. In 1867 he patented his new explosive "dynamite." By 1880 he was head of one of the largest dynamite producing cartels in the world.

And then one day a simple mistake changed his life forever. In 1888, the death of his brother Ludvig caused several newspapers to publish obituaries of Alfred in error. A French obituary stated "Le marchand de la mort est mort" ("The merchant of death is dead"). Due to this error, Alfred got the opportunity to do what lots of people would like to do. He was able to read his own obituary and saw what people had made of his life. But he read phrases like "merchant of death" and "that his fortune was amassed finding new ways to mutilate and kill."

As Nobel held the newspaper in his hands, he vowed that this was not how he should be remembered, and he decided that, from that very day, his life wouldn't just be successful but significant. He began using his vast wealth to encourage the arts, science and above all peace. This was the origin of the Nobel peace prize.

Few who have watched people collect the Nobel Peace prize, as Nelson Mandella did in 1995, will realise that the event was due to the error of journalists. Their simple mistakes changed another man's life forever and in doing so changed many other people's lives too.

It's possible for people to be very self-critical for a long period of time about their mistakes and fail to forgive themselves. Mistakes are part of life and inevitable. As the poet Alexander Pope so accurately said "To err is human; to forgive divine."

Many people that I've coached over the years have been very hard on themselves and needed some help to let go of mistakes they were holding onto. It's easy to fall into this trap of repeating these incidents in our minds, to focus on what has gone wrong and didn't work out the way we planned. As opposed to focusing on what's right and is going well. This can mean that we limit what we achieve in life. As shown in Nobel's story not all mistakes are bad and learning how to use them to your advantage is a positive personal habit to develop.

When we make mistakes it's an opportunity to learn and deepen our knowledge. Such situations can help us discover hidden depths in ourselves. Mistakes give us the chance to figure out what we really like and value in life. They also help us clarify what's important to us. Although they can be painful and lead to a difficult period to navigate they can help us to grow. A great habit to get into following a mistake is to ask yourself "What is this teaching me?"

It's also important to remember that our mistakes don't define us as a person as they are just a snapshot of our life. We're much more than our challenges or past mistakes. Sadly, some people don't achieve all that they could in life because they procrastinate and become paralysed by a fear of making a mistake or experiencing failure.

Thomas Edison didn't see his 10,000 attempts to invent the light bulb as failures. He saw them as discoveries of ways that didn't work and moved him closer to a solution.

I often say to clients when they are contemplating change and a new approach that there is no failure only feedback, to not fear mistakes and to go for it.

**Reflection time:**

Pause for a few moments and reflect on the following questions:

What mistakes you or others have made do you need to let go and forgive?

What did these mistakes teach you?

## 14. Be willing to be flexible

> "Those who cannot change their minds cannot change anything." George Bernard Shaw.

A recent coaching client talked about when he has a heavy workload, gets stressed and feels under pressure. He told me he becomes very single minded and inflexible in his approach to tasks and sticks rigidly to his ideas and plans

We discussed the impact of this approach on him and his relationships with others. He told me that it can make his vision very tunnelled and can stop him listening to the input and valuable ideas of others. He becomes defensive which has an impact on his relationships with others who tend to distance themselves and keep their heads down.

He said that he found it extremely challenging to show his vulnerability and admit he made a mistake and traced this back to his upbringing. He told me that he sometimes gets so caught up in a goal that he becomes unwilling to let go of it even when he knows deep down that the existing plans won't work. He conceded that it came down to a need to be seen to be right.

He said that he wanted to change this particular pattern of behaviour as it made him unhappy and no longer served him. He sought my help to do so. I shared the following story to demonstrate what can happen when we are too rigid in our thinking and how having a willingness to change direction can be beneficial.

On a dark and foggy night in the midst of a stormy sea, the captain of a ship spotted what seemed to be the light from another ship in the distance. He quickly went to his station and flashed a message across the water, "change your course twenty degrees north." No sooner had he done this than a reply flashed back, "change your course twenty degrees south." The captain became angry and flashed back, "I am captain and a commander in the naval forces, and I say change your course twenty degrees north." The responding message was signalled back, "I am a seaman first class with no commander, and I say change your course twenty degrees south." This infuriated the captain who now signalled, "I am a battleship, and I say change your course twenty degrees north." There was a brief pause as the angry captain awaited the reply. Finally, the response came, "I say change your course twenty degrees south, I am a lighthouse!"

The story struck a chord with my client and he resolved to adopt a different approach to life and set about devising some actions to change some behavioural patterns. The story also gave him a powerful metaphor to refer to and remind him when he felt that he was slipping back into his old way of being.

In my experience, the people with the most flexible approach to goals, relationships and life in general, tend to be happier and enjoy a greater connection with others. They accept situations as they are and focus on what's going right in their lives. They don't spend time wishing that the past had turned out differently. They adapt to new situations easily, welcome the adventure of trying something new, learning different perspectives and meeting new people. They avoid getting defensive and can think on their feet, willing to change direction if the situation dictates it.

You can develop your mental flexibility by reviewing what you do in life particularly those things that are habitual. You can ask yourself the question "what is the purpose of what I am doing and is it really necessary?" It's possible to develop a more open minded approach to change by changing your routine.

For instance, you could try a different route to work, establish a new time to go to bed and start getting up earlier. You can use the additional time for exercise or personal development. If you always chair particular meetings, you could rotate the role to others and suggest a different format to the agenda to avoid it becoming the same old same old.

You can also make a conscious effort to look at situations and issues from other people's perspective. Being open to other people's ideas can change your thinking and help you to experience new and exciting things in life.

**Reflection time:**

Pause for a few moments and reflect on the following questions:

Do you need to change your plans and approach to a particular goal or project?

What would be the benefit of doing so and what motivates you to make a change?

## 15. Every day is a gift

**"The best gift we can have is living in the present moment and really enjoying it for what it is; and, not being in our heads and getting side-tracked." Amy Smart.**

In July 2014 like many people across the world I was shocked and deeply saddened to hear about the shooting down of Malaysia Airlines Flight 17 (MH17). This killed all 283 passengers and 15 crew on board. It was a scheduled international passenger flight from Amsterdam to Kuala Lumpur International airport. It was a truly horrific and senseless tragedy and I struggled to understand and comprehend how it could have happened and why.

Incidents like this are a reminder to us all that life is fragile and none of us know what's around the corner. It also re-affirms that we must strive to not sweat the small stuff and to avoid getting anxious, frustrated or angry about things that don't really matter. It teaches us to not get irritated when we are kept waiting or if we have to queue in a shop. It makes you wonder why we get stressed when someone is late for an appointment, if we miss a deadline or we encounter a traffic jam etc.

It's important that we treat every day as a gift, to learn to live and enjoy the present moment. Irrespective of what happened yesterday or may or may not happen tomorrow, the present moment is where we are - always!

I once saw a poster outside the British Library in London, which has stuck with me – it contained a quote by Eleanor Roosevelt and said "yesterday is history, tomorrow is a mystery, today is a gift that's why we call it the present."

The sad events described above are a reminder to us all about what truly matters in life – loved ones, family, good friendships, good health, the things we're passionate about and bring joy to us and others. It's so vitally important that we have balance in our lives. The following story is a great metaphor with a powerful message about priorities and what matters most in life.

**Rocks, Pebbles and Sand**

A philosophy professor stood before his class with some items in front of him. When class began, he wordlessly picked up a large empty mayonnaise jar and proceeded to fill it with rocks about two inches in diameter. He then asked the students if the jar was full. They agreed that it was.

The professor then picked up a box of pebbles, poured them into the jar and lightly shook it. The pebbles, of course, rolled into the open areas between the rocks. The students laughed. He asked his students again if the jar was full. They agreed that it was.

The professor then picked up a box of sand and poured it into the jar. Of course, the sand filled up everything else.

"Now," said the professor, "I want you to recognize that this is your life. The rocks are the important things—your family, your partner, your health, your children—anything that is so important to you that if it were lost, you would be nearly destroyed. The pebbles are the other things in life that matter, but on a smaller scale. The pebbles represent things like your job, your house, your car. The sand is everything else—the small stuff".

"If you put the sand or the pebbles into the jar first, there is no room for the rocks. The same goes for your life. If you spend all your energy and time on the small stuff, material things, you will never have room for the things that are truly most important. Pay attention to the things that are critical in your life. Play with your children. Take your partner out dancing. There will always be time to go to work, clean the house, give a dinner party and fix the rubbish. In your own life, be sure to take care of the rocks first—the things that really matter. Remember, the rest is only pebbles and sand."

Finally after everyone agreed the jar was now full, he picked up a glass of wine and proceeded to pour it into jar. Of course the wine filled the remaining spaces within the jar making the jar truly full. He told the class that the alternative message was no matter how full your life is there's always room for a glass of fine wine!

**Reflection time:**

Pause for a few moments and reflect on the following questions:

Is there any action you need to take to make more time for the "rocks" in your life?

What changes (if any) do you need to make to your daily schedule?

## 16. Lessons for effective teamwork from the Red Arrows

### "Alone we can do so little; together we can do so much." Helen Keller.

I watched a fascinating documentary about life behind the scenes of the RAF Red Arrows aerobatics team. It provided a unique insight into the work of the 120 pilots, support and ground crew as they prepared to celebrate their 50th display season.

It was filmed in Cyprus as they underwent 6 months of training building up to an assessment day, where it was decided if the team were up to the requisite standard to fly in public displays. It's a high stakes day, where they are either cleared to fly or judged not to be ready.

The team had 9 pilots, 2 of which were new recruits under training. The new recruits were experienced elite pilots, the best of the best but they faced the most gruelling six months of their lives. Each said all they thought about from sunrise to sunset was the training. They said it was a more stressful experience than the dangerous missions they'd been involved in previously. They would either fulfil a childhood dream or face heartbreak. The training was relentless, 3 flights daily, 5 days a week, with each flight forensically analysed.

Five possible new recruits for future years joined the team for a week just before the assessment day in Cyprus. In addition to flying, they undergo interviews with all the team. They attend social events which are closely observed to see how they interact with others.

I have detailed below some insights all teams can learn from the Red Arrows:

**Trust**

Trust is the foundation and critical when building a high performing team. You need to be able to count on your team-mates to be there for you when you need help. It's vital that you trust their abilities and appreciate the contribution that they make to the team results. Trust is particularly important for the Red Arrows given the dangerous nature of what they do – flying sometimes at 400 miles an hour just 6 feet apart!

**Clear purpose and plan**

It's important that everyone clearly understands the purpose and objectives of the team. A detailed plan of how you'll get there and the role each member has to play to execute the plan is useful. A back up and contingency plan that can be introduced swiftly if there's an unforeseen incident is also helpful.

**Constructive feedback and commitment to improvement**

After all flights, pilots participate in a detailed, forensic debrief which includes video footage of the flight. They employ a clever psychological trick in the briefing room to avoid conflict. They never refer to each other by name. Instead they use Red 1 through to Red 9. Whilst having personal opinions, the team must get on with each other as conflict and tension isn't something they can accommodate. Practice and training is crucial to keep the team on the ball. Even the best performers need to be committed to learning new things, practising and honing their skills.

## Recruitment and selection

The pilots are selected for their professionalism, skills and teamwork. Lots of time is invested in considering how people will fit in and gel with each other. It teaches us that it's best to listen to and trust our instincts if we feel that someone isn't the right fit. This will avoid having to deal problems later on. It's important for a team leader to be very clear about the standards and behaviours they expect from their team. Setting the right tone and environment from the outset can't be overstated.

## Focused competitive team players

The Red Arrows team manager said they look for competitive people but nice rather than bad competitive. They want people who have a will to be the best but are also team players who can fit in and encourage that in others. They must maintain good levels of trust with their fellow pilots and can't be competing with each other in the air.

## Honest and open communication

They call a spade a spade in the briefing room. Opinions are offered in the spirit that as a team they are looking to be the best they can be. Errors are pointed out and suggestions to correct them made. The views expressed aren't personal.

## Reflection time:

Pause for a few moments and reflect on the following question:

What could the teams or groups that you are involved in do differently to become more effective?

## 17. Don't wait for the right tools and circumstances

> "Twenty years from now you will be more disappointed by the things that you didn't do than by the ones you did. So throw off the bowlines. Sail away from the safe harbour. Catch the trade winds in your sails. Explore. Dream. Discover." Mark Twain.

Seve Ballesteros is one of my all-time sporting heroes. I therefore enjoyed watching "Seve the Movie" which tells his life story.

I found the film both inspiring and incredibly moving. Inspiring, because it provided evidence that if you have a big enough desire and commit yourself to achieving your dream, you can overcome the odds and achieve anything. Moving because he died so young in May 2011 aged just 54. Sadly, Seve was diagnosed with a brain tumour in 2008, a year after he retired from golf and ultimately it caused his premature death.

Despite being blocked at almost every turn in pursuit of the sport he loved, Seve fought against adversity to become one of the most talented, exciting and charismatic golfers to ever play the game.

He was a genius with a golf club in his hands, an inspiration to everyone who saw him create shots that didn't seem possible. The Spaniard's passion and pride revived European golf and made the Ryder Cup one of the game's most compelling events. Ballesteros, a five-time major champion had an incomparable imagination and fiery personality. His career was defined not only by what he won, but how he won. He was feisty. He was proud. He was charming. He made people watch, and he usually gave them something to remember.

Seve played with a rare combination of talent and heart, and his intensity endeared him to his teammates in the Ryder Cup, a competition that elevated his talent and leadership. He once said, "I would like to be remembered as an artist, someone who made the people happy."

When Seve died the legendary golfer, Jack Nicklaus said. "Today, golf lost a great champion and a great friend. We also lost a great entertainer and ambassador for our sport, no matter the golf that particular day, you always knew you were going to be entertained. Seve's enthusiasm was just unmatched by anybody I think that ever played the game."

He started life in humble beginnings. His parents ran a small holding in Pedrana, Northern Spain and didn't have a great deal of money. He was the youngest of 5 boys. He developed a passion for golf early in life. Aged 9 he practised golf daily on the beach using a make shift club made from a rusty 3 iron. He had a vision to be the best golfer the world had ever seen. His passion and love of the game meant that he skipped school and dedicated himself to developing and honing his skill. Partly because of his humble roots, partly because of his Spanish blood, Ballesteros always played as though he had something to prove.

The story gives some valuable insights to anyone that has a dream that they would like to realise which I summarise below:

- A lack of the right tools, equipment and environment doesn't need to hold you back. Remember Seve learnt his trade with a make shift club and on a beach.
- The power of visualisation. If you have a clear vision and strong enough desire you will achieve your dream.
- The importance of practice and commitment. Each day you need to do something to progress your goal and improve your performance and skills. Nothing comes easily but is achievable with small consistent steps.
- Adversity and setbacks don't need to define you. Seve was expelled from school and his parents couldn't afford for him to play at the local golf club full time. They once sold a prize calf to raise money for him to play a vital match which he won against the odds.
- Life is short and it's important that we follow our heart, seize our opportunities and spend time doing things we love and are passionate about.
- It's never too late to pursue your dream – it starts with a single step and that is often the hardest one to take.

**Reflection time:**

Pause for a few moments and reflect on the following questions:

What are you passionate about that you would like to spend more time doing?

Is there something you'd like to learn or a new hobby you'd like to pursue?

## 18. Persistence pays off

**"Patience, persistence and perspiration make an unbeatable combination for success." Napoleon Hill.**

I'm often asked what I consider to be the most important qualities required to attain success. This isn't an easy question to answer given there isn't a single definition for success. We're all unique, have different talents and life experiences and have our own personal success definition.

There are many traits required to help people to be successful at what they set out to do. It's rare for there to be a straight line to a successful outcome. Along the way we encounter opposition, have to overcome obstacles and bounce back from set-backs and unexpected events.

Some of the most successful people in history had to overcome adversity and keep faith with what they were seeking to achieve (some examples are given in chapter 23). I believe a quality that's required to be successful is persistence. The dictionary defines persistence as "the quality that allows someone to continue doing something or trying to do something even though it is difficult or opposed by other people."

Persistence helps turn something we visualise or imagine and turn it into a reality. Persistence enables us to learn, develop and acquire new knowledge. When combined with sustained effort and fine tuning it ensures we accomplish our goals.

When we set out to achieve something in life we're often given a series of tests which enable us to discover hidden strengths and

- 1849 - Sought the job of land officer in his home state – rejected.
- 1854 - Ran for Senate of the United States – lost.
- 1856 - Sought the Vice-Presidential nomination at his party's national convention – got less than 100 votes.
- 1858 - Ran for U.S. Senate again – again he lost.
- 1860 - Elected president of the United States(inaugurated March 1861).

**Reflection time:**

Pause for a few moments and reflect on the following question:

Is there something in your life that requires more persistence on your part or a slight change of approach?

## 19. Play to your strengths

> "Success is achieved by developing our strengths, not by eliminating our weaknesses." **Marilyn Vos Savant.**

When I start coaching a new client we begin with a "getting to know you" session. As part of this process, I ask clients to tell me about themselves. Most people start by telling me what they aren't very good at and what they don't want to experience or achieve in life.

Interestingly, very few people begin by describing what they are good at and what they want to experience and achieve in life. It's very rare for people to be able to articulate their top strengths. Most people are generally modest and reluctant to talk about their strengths. However, they can easily detail their weaknesses or development needs.

Why are we conditioned to think and talk in this way? In doing so, we may be denying ourselves the opportunity to grow and realise our potential. It's possible that we adopt this approach because we're encouraged at an early age to work hard on our weak areas and things that we aren't good at.

I guess that another reason may be because there's so much negativity in our cultures. We have school reports that highlight areas for improvement, annual performance reviews that are slanted towards development needs. There are also advertisements that play on people's fears and promote products that address a problem. I often wonder what people are missing out on in life by focusing their attention on negatives and improvements.

What impact does it have on the productivity and profitability of businesses by failing to focus on their employee's strengths? For many years, I've held the view that one of the vital roles of a leader is to identify and nurture their team's strengths and ensure that they put round pegs in round holes.

We all have strengths and natural talents as well as areas where we're not so strong.  Having a clear understanding of our strengths helps us to build self - esteem and confidence. It enables us to have a greater appreciation of the value that we bring to tasks, teams and other people.

I often ask clients what the effect on their results and life would be if they had clarity on their core strengths and played to them. Instead of expending time and effort focused on what they aren't good at and what's not working.

I've found that when people gain a greater understanding of their strengths and the value they bring to the world they experience greater happiness, fulfilment and increased self-worth. Surely that's sufficient motivation and incentive to gain more personal insight in this area.

Imagine the impact on companies and society in general, if all teams had a greater appreciation of their own and colleague's strengths and were encouraged to play to them.  I'm sure there would be higher employee satisfaction and engagement levels, uplift in customer satisfaction and results. Working environments would be more positive and energised.

I recommend you dedicate some time developing a list of your top 5 strengths. Once you've gained this clarity you can devise some concrete action steps to ensure you use them more often.

I've found that some people don't find it easy to come up with their own list. Where it's proving to be testing, I encourage them to seek input from family members, colleagues or friends. It's best to approach people who know you well and can be trusted to give helpful, supportive and honest feedback. Quite often others see our positive qualities and contributions more easily than we do ourselves.

This process helps shine a light on blind spots and helps to positively build self-awareness. You can ask those closest to you to answer the following questions:

- What do you think is the most interesting thing about me?
- What do you value most about me?
- What do you perceive to be my greatest strengths?

If you want to use external resources to gain insight, the Clifton strengths finder assessment takes about 30 minutes to complete online. It will provide you with your top 5 strengths and a detailed summary. It costs US $15 (about £10) and can be purchased at www.gallupstrengthscenter.com/Purchase/

**Reflection time:**

Pause for a few moments and reflect on the following questions:

What are your greatest strengths?

What action can you take to ensure that you make the most of your natural gifts and talents?

## 20. Watch your self talk & keep it positive

**"Once you replace negative thoughts with positive ones, you'll start having positive results." Willie Nelson.**

I was astonished when I first discovered some research that suggested that the average person talks to him/herself about 60,000 times a day. Furthermore it's said that most of this self-talk is negative.

That's an awful lot of chatter that goes on sub consciously. Apparently this kind of internal chatter is connected to lots of self judgement and criticism. Examples may include:-

I'm too old to learn something new, I shouldn't have made that comment, I'm sure he/she doesn't like me, I'm not equipped to jog every day, I will never lose weight, I don't like the way my hair looks, I'm useless with computers, I can't do this task etc.

It's important that we pay more attention to our inner chatter. What we say to ourselves is just as important as what we say to others. Our self- talk has a major influence and drives our behaviour. Therefore if we tell ourselves that we can't do something or that we're unable to master a new skill, our behaviour will reflect this fact and belief. It becomes a self-fulfilling prophecy and shapes the results that we experience.

Imagine you are given a task to sell 60 units of widgets in a week. If you tell yourself from the outset that you can't do it, you will spend time and energy behaving in a way that proves this thought and belief to be correct. As human beings we like to be proved right, even if our belief is misguided. If you expect failure you will get a 100% success rate.

If on the other hand, you believe and confidently expect to sell 60 units in a week you're more likely to achieve the result you expect. Your self-talk will be positive, encouraging and affirming. This will lead your behaviour to be more energised, positive and optimistic. As a result you're more likely to achieve the results that you expect and desire.

The self-talk occurs through the conscious area of our mind and become instructions to our sub-conscious mind whose duty is to carry out the orders given to it by the conscious part of our brain.

I was given the following metaphor to help me understand how the two minds work and the relationship between them. Imagine that a navy ship is crossing the Atlantic Ocean. The captain of the ship is located on the bridge on the upper deck and gives orders to the crew who are located in the lower deck, below the water line and are unable to see where the ship is going.

In this example, the captain is the conscious mind and the crew the sub-conscious mind. When the captain provides an order about the direction the ship should travel in and the speed, the crew carry out the orders. They don't have a clue if the ship will avoid colliding with another vessel, run aground or safely reach its destination. It's not their role to determine. Their role is just to carry out the instructions without questioning them or passing judgement. Given this metaphor, if we want to make an improvement in any part of our life, it's essential that we ensure our self-talk is positive.

Negative thoughts and self- talk have a physical impact on our body. They make us feel heavy, weighed down and can deplete our energy. Negative self-talk can make us feel frightened, anxious, cause us to break out into a sweat or become tongue tied.

If we talked to ourselves in a more encouraging way, what would this do to our physical well-being and results?

Here are some tips on using more positive language:

- Replace the word "can't" with "can" i.e. "I can do this."
- Substitute the word "never" with "sometimes." "I never get these sums right" could be softened by saying "I sometimes get these sums right."
- "Should" is a negative word used in self judgment – when you find yourself saying " I should" to yourself, change it to the word "could." "I should be good at golf," can be changed to "I could be good at golf." The latter has a more encouraging feel to it.
- Eradicate the word "try" from your vocabulary. You will either do something or not do it. You don't try and do it. For instance do you try and move a chair or do you just move it or not bother?

**Reflection time:**

Pause for a moment and reflect on the following questions:

How encouraging is your self-talk?

Do you need to change any of your inner dialogue?

## 21. Practice gratitude and increase your happiness

**"Let us be grateful to the people who make us happy; they are the charming gardeners who make our souls blossom."
Marcel Proust.**

It's easy for us all to fall into the trap of focusing our mind on what we lack, what's not working and what's wrong with our life. Falling into this habit doesn't help our energy levels, mood or assist us to maintain a positive outlook. In today's fast paced world with countless demands and distractions, we can all easily forget and overlook the things to be grateful for in life.

For instance, we can take for granted that at the turn of a tap we have fresh running water to drink and wash in. We can overlook that at the flick of a switch we have electricity to power the kettle to make a hot drink and listen to the radio when we wake up. The electricity or gas supply also means we can take a hot shower or bath.

Being more deliberate about practising gratitude and acknowledging all that there is to be grateful for in life helps keep energy levels high, leads to happy and positive feelings. It enables us to be better equipped to deal with challenges and hassles that we all inevitably face from time to time.

When I first started deliberately practising this approach, I wrote a list of 50 things to be grateful for which I added to over the course of a month. I still refer to this list from time to time when things don't go as planned, if I am facing an obstacle or if my energy level drops. It always lifts my spirits and puts things into balance and perspective. After reading the list, I remind myself that whatever issue I am facing "this too will pass." I find that it is a bit like pressing a reset button on the computer and returns life to smoother running.

Another practice that I've found helpful is to take the time to acknowledge positive events when they happen. I make a note of such events on post it notes which I put in a jar. I note down special family time, acts of kindness, positive feedback, receipt of income, gifts, unexpected windfalls, great customer service and nice experiences such as days out, time by the sea, special restaurant meals, going to a concert, sporting events etc.

At the end of each year, I take out the notes and read them all. I've found this to be an excellent way to acknowledge and appreciate all the things that I have been fortunate to experience during that year, as I prepare and look forward to the New Year.

Robert A. Emmons & Michael McCullough are two of the leading scholars on the topic of gratitude and they have researched and written about its power to boost happiness. In one of their studies, they carried out research with 3 experimental groups over a 10 week period.

1. The first group was asked to write down five things they were grateful for that had happened in the last week for each of the 10 weeks of the study. This was called the gratitude condition.

2. The second group was asked to write down five daily hassles from the previous week. This was the hassles condition.

3. The third group simply listed five events that had occurred in the last week, but not told to focus on positive or negative aspects. This was the events or control condition.

Before the experiment began participants had kept daily journals to chronicle their moods, physical health and general attitudes. These were then used to provide a comparison for after the experimental intervention.

People who were in the gratitude condition felt fully 25% happier. They were more optimistic about the future, they felt better about their lives and they even did almost 1.5 hours more exercise a week than those in the hassles or events condition.

Martin Seligman is a leading expert on positive psychology and a very successful author. He has looked extensively at the effect and benefits of practising gratitude in his work. He has found that writing down what you are grateful for has the ability to shape your mood positively in lasting ways.

**Reflection time:**

Pause for a few moments and consider the following question:

What are you grateful for in life? (Aim for a list of 50 things and then add to it over the coming month).

## 22. Dealing with obstacles

> "Stand up to your obstacles and do something about them. You will find that they haven't half the strength you think they have." Norman Vincent Peale.

We're are all born with unlimited potential but on occasions we simply get in our own way and make life more complicated than it really needs to be. There's a great quotation by Confucius, "Life is really simple, but we insist on making it complicated!" Sometimes the biggest limitations we have in life are the ones that we impose on ourselves and have in our own minds.

During my coaching skills training, I was taught a very simple but powerful formula that I've subsequently used with thousands of people. It helps to easily identify and deal with the obstacles that stop us from being the very best that we can be. The formula is:-

### Performance = Potential – Interference

It was devised by Timothy Gallwey who had previously worked as a tennis coach. Gallwey says that on a tennis court the biggest opponent isn't the one you are playing against but the one up in your own head and is part of the foundation for the formula.

Gallwey has written a series of books in which he has set forth a new methodology for coaching and for the development of personal and professional excellence in a variety of fields, that he calls "The Inner Game." His book "The Inner Game of Work" is all about helping people overcoming mental obstacles for maximum performance. Some of the other books he has written include "The Inner Game of Tennis" and "The Inner Game of Golf."

Gallwey claimed that performance in any activity, from hitting a tennis ball to solving a complex business problem, was equal to one's potential after the interference factor had been subtracted from the equation. Performance rarely equals potential. A little interference is all it takes to greatly diminish one's actual performance. Some common examples of interferences (obstacles) are self- doubt, fear, lack of confidence, self-condemnation and negative self –talk, perfectionism, trying too hard, lack of willpower, boredom, anger, frustration, procrastination, self-consciousness, busy mind, assumptions, lack of focus, no goals and lack of direction.

One of the biggest interferences is fear or as I like to call it "False Expectations Appearing Real!" There are many fears that stop people fulfilling their potential and goals. These include fear of rejection which stops people asking for what they want, a fear of criticism which prevents people attempting a new approach to a task. A fear of change and the unknown keeps some stuck in their comfort zone. A fear of success for some individuals means they self sabotage their results so that they continue to mesh with the crowd.

I was once told we're born with just two fears - the fear of noise and falling down. Every other fear we have is a learned behaviour. The good news about interferences including fear is that as they are a learned behaviour, we can unlearn them! It requires us to form some new habits and behaviours. Changing our daily habits and rituals is the starting point that allows us to get out of our own way.

Obstacles do present us with an opportunity to learn and grow as we discover new depths as we search for solutions to overcome them.

We may discover that we are more creative than we realised when we devise solutions that are new and innovative. This can help develop our self-confidence and self-worth.

Self-belief can increase when we face and overcome our obstacles. Faith in our ability when confronted with an obstacle is a great habit to develop.

Adopting a positive mindset to interferences and obstacles is another great quality to hone. As is, believing that obstacles however inconvenient are an opportunity to gain new knowledge and gain experience. Overcoming interferences provides a sense of accomplishment and is a useful future reference point when faced with similar challenges.

**Reflection time:**

Pause for a few moments and reflect on the following questions:

In what ways do you get in your own way?

Are there any interferences or obstacles that you need to overcome?

What resources and people are available to support you with any changes that you would like to make?

## 23. Don't let adversity & setbacks hold you back

**"If we did all the things that we are capable of doing, we would literally astound ourselves." Thomas Edison.**

Thomas Edison is regarded as one of the most successful inventors of all time. He invented an astonishing 1,093 things including the phonograph (early version of a record player), motion picture camera and the incandescent light bulb. In fact, as I mentioned earlier in the book, it's reported that it took him 10,000 attempts to create the lightbulb.

Edison is featured in a book, "People who changed the world." His achievements are even more remarkable given that he had little formal education; he was expelled from school because his teachers thought he had learning difficulties. In fact he suffered from hearing problems throughout his life. Edison's enormous achievements were entirely due to years of hard work and his natural intelligence. It's interesting how he didn't allow his teacher's judgements to hold him back.

We all face adversity, challenges, obstacles, frustrations and setbacks at times in our lives. When in the middle of periods of misfortune or challenge it's easy to lose perspective, become downhearted and wonder if things will ever improve. It can have a detrimental effect on our levels of confidence and belief. Sometimes we have to experience difficulty and tough times so that we can develop a greater appreciation of the good times and be grateful for the periods of pleasure.

When you set out to achieve a goal or a dream, whether it is starting a business, pursuing a new career, beginning a new hobby, looking to lose weight or commencing a fitness regime, it's easy at the first sign of a setback to give up and settle for what's known.

There are countless examples of the challenges that people encountered on the road to success. We may never have heard a record from the Beatles, if they had taken rejection as a sign to not pursue their passion. When they first started out, a recording company turned them down and said "we don't like your sound and guitar music is on the way out."

Many people may not have viewed a Disney movie or visited Disneyworld if Walt Disney had given up when he was fired early in his career by a newspaper editor because "he lacked imagination and had no good ideas." He suffered business failure, bankruptcy and was turned down an incredible 302 times by banks when he was seeking funds to establish his theme park. He never gave up on his dream to create Disneyworld. It took him years of hard work, raising finance, dealing with disappointment but Disney stayed focused on his goal.

The Harry Potter movies and JK Rowling's books are hugely popular across the world with lots of people. They may have been denied that pleasure; if she had let difficulties she experienced in life hold her back. Prior to the books being published, she was virtually penniless, depending on welfare payments to survive and help to bring up her child as a single parent. She was divorced and suffered from depression. Her series of seven books has since sold more than 450 million copies, won innumerable awards, been made into movies, and transformed Rowling's life.

Oprah Winfrey faced a hard road to be one of the most iconic faces on television. It has been written that she endured a rough and often abusive childhood as well as numerous career setbacks including being fired from her job as a television reporter because she was "unfit for television."

Richard Branson is one of the richest men in the UK and hasn't let his dyslexia hold him back in life. He left school at 15 with no qualifications. Instead of giving up, he used the power of his personality to drive him to success and create his Virgin empire.

Experiencing adversity can be a lesson. It can re-awaken us to the things that are far more important than money and material possessions; our health, our family and our friends. An illness teaches us to be humble, to see every day as a gift, to live more in the moment and motivate us to lead a healthy life. A sudden loss in the family brings into sharp focus the cycle of birth, life and death.

Adversity can come to our lives to suggest that it's time for us to change direction and do something new. For instance, job loss can be a scary place and create uncertainty but it can be the springboard for something new and exciting and the start of a whole new adventure.

**Reflection time:**

Pause for a few moments and reflect on the following question:

What lessons have challenges and adversity taught you?

## 24. Put yourself first sometimes

> "To keep a lamp burning we have to keep putting oil in it."
> Mother Theresa.

In a recent coaching session, a client who runs her own very successful business and is always upbeat and appears in control confided in me that she felt close to burn out. She has high standards and produces outstanding results and it took a lot of courage for her to admit the truth about how she was feeling inside. She was struggling to balance the demands of her business with her home life and parental responsibilities.

She told me that she felt it was imperative that she developed some new habits as her current way of being wasn't enjoyable or sustainable. We live in an information rich and time poor world. Increasingly, I'm seeing examples of people feeling overwhelmed, struggling to juggle different priorities, sustain high performance levels and lead happy balanced lives.

The objective that my client set for the coaching session was to discover how she could sustain and develop her current performance levels and avoid health problems. She was very honest and admitted to me that the main lesson that she gained from the current challenge was that she needed to ask for help more often and not feel weak or guilty for doing so.

During our chat, I mentioned a metaphor that I had learned by boarding a plane. Have you noticed that when they make the safety announcement the crew always give a specific instruction? They tell you that in the event of an emergency (when the oxygen mask appears) to apply your mask first. They say that you must do this before you attempt to help others with their mask. The reason for this is that if you don't have any oxygen/energy you won't be in a position to help others.

My client told me in that instant that she realised it was time for her to apply her oxygen mask and increase her energy levels. She needed to take action and look after her needs more than she had done in the past.

Sometimes we have to put ourselves first so that we can be the best we can be and have the energy to help others. Many people put others needs in front of their own, as they feel it self-indulgent to put themselves first. They feel that by doing so it's at odds with how they were taught in childhood not to be selfish.

The key to this is to have balance between the amount that you care for others and your needs. Being well rested and looking after your health means that you have the requisite energy you need to help those around you. If you're regularly tired because you have irregular sleep patterns, skip meals or fail to get some exercise, then start making these things an absolute priority.

The phrase self-care has gained in popularity over recent years and reminds us of the importance of taking care of our needs, so we can be the best that we can be. It prompts us to take care of our physical needs (getting enough sleep, right diet, exercise etc.); emotional needs (asking for help when needed); mental needs (stimulating job, interests, personal development etc.); spiritual needs (time for prayer, meditation etc.).

**Here are a few self-care tips:**

- Keep hydrated by drinking plenty of water. The recommended daily limit is 1.5-2 litres a day.
- Eat 5 pieces of fruit and vegetables daily.
- Exercise – it's recommended that you undertake 30 minutes of physical exercise daily. This doesn't have to be a visit to a gym as a brisk walk is good for you.

- Ensure that you get enough sleep to give your body time to relax and recover. The amount of sleep each person needs varies but on average it is 8 hours a night. Keep your sleep patterns regular by going to bed and getting up at the same times every day. Avoid using the snooze button!
- Minimise the amount of caffeine that you have on a daily basis and keep alcohol intake within the recommended weekly limits.
- Be more disciplined with your time. Learn to say no, be more assertive and protect your boundaries.
- Set time aside daily (even if it's just 10 minutes) to relax your mind through meditation or mindfulness.
- Regularly watch funny movies/comedies to have a good laugh. Humour helps you feel good, more relaxed and happier.
- Avoid negative people and environments that drain your energy. Be more discerning about how you spend your energy.

**Reflection time:**

Pause for a few moments and reflect on the following questions:

What action do you need to take to put your needs first more often?

What do you need to do to create more energy and balance in your life?

## 25. Where are you investing your energy?

> "A pessimist sees the difficulty in every opportunity; an optimist sees the opportunity in every difficulty."
> **Sir Winston Churchill.**

In the previous chapter, I talked about putting your needs first sometimes to deal with overwhelm and having to balance many priorities. I mentioned the importance of doing this to keep your energy levels high. In this chapter, I'm going to look at the subject of energy and creating some additional space and time.

As I get older, I'm becoming more discerning about how I invest my energy and who I spend my time with. When I am around the vibe given off by pessimistic, complaining and negative people it starts to have a real impact on my energy levels. My body starts to feel heavy, I feel tired and drained.

I know that we all have challenges and problems from time to time and life isn't always a bed of roses. In the face of difficulty and adversity, it isn't easy for people to remain upbeat. It's important we offer support to those with genuine challenges and problems to solve.

What I'm referring to are the perennial moaners and negative people. You've probably come across these people yourself. They believe that "every silver lining has a cloud" and refer constantly to their problems and don't look for solutions. Often they have much to be grateful for but they don't recognise this. They choose to think about what they lack rather than the abundance they have.

When you ask them how they are, they hunch their shoulders and say something like "fair to grim" and launch into a detailed account of their troubles. I refer to them as "drains or energy vampires" because they suck the life out of you with their negativity and stories of how life is unfair! More frequently, I am choosing to give them a wide berth.

Conversely, I have noticed that when I'm around positive people (those that give off a positive vibe) with a "can do" attitude and solutions orientated approach, I feel lighter, energised and happier. I refer to these people as "radiators" as they are full of warmth, radiance and brightness. They have zest, vitality and they make the most of the hand that life has dealt them. When you ask them how they are, they look you in the eye; they smile and say something positive and uplifting. They have a sense of gratitude and appreciation for what they have in life.

An exercise that I recommend is to take an A4 piece of paper and draw a line down the centre. On the left hand side draw a positive sign and right hand side a negative sign. Ask yourself the question "what people/activities give me energy?" Note down your responses under the positive sign. Then ask yourself, what people/activities drain my energy?" Note your responses under the negative sign. Review your results and decide if you need to make any changes to the way you spend your time.

In this information rich, time poor world there are many potential sources of distractions and demands on our time. Technology is amazing however it brings its challenges. It's said that the conscious brain can only handle 7 bits of information at any one time and is a reason why we can feel overloaded at times.

The overwhelmed feeling can also prevent us from starting new pursuits as we feel we don't have sufficient time or mental capacity to take on anything new. When clients are feeling this way I recommend they look at ways to create more space and time.

I suggest that they spend some time considering what they can STOP doing to create some space for some new habits and behaviours and provide some room for growth. Clients who have compiled a STOP doing lists tell me that it gave them greater clarity, helped to sharpen their focus and gave them renewed energy. They say that it allowed them to concentrate on their most important and rewarding activities. Clients normally complete lists for both their personal and professional lives. Here are a few common examples of what clients choose to STOP doing at work:

- Using " reply all" with e mail
- Checking social network sites
- Using e mail alerts/notifications
- Checking e mail outside of designated time slots
- Holding meetings with no agenda or clear objectives or doing recaps for late arrivals
- Failing to preserve uninterrupted time for important work projects

**Reflection time:**

Pause for a few moments and reflect on the following questions:

What people/activities give you energy?

What activities/people drain your energy?

What can you stop doing to create some space?

## 26. Always Be First Class – the A-Z for personal and professional success and fulfilment

**"Always do your best. What you plant now, you will harvest later." Go Mandino.**

As we've reached the half-way point of the book, I thought we'd take a bit of a breather and reflect on some of the key messages in the book. To do this, I have included a list that I compiled at the start of 2016. The A-Z of Always Being First Class is as a collection of tips about some of the healthy habits, behaviours and mindset that I recommend you adopt to be the best you can be. I hope it helps to bring personal and professional success and happiness to you.

- **A**sk for and accept help when you need it.
- **B**alance time between work and play.
- **C**elebrate your successes and accomplishments.
- **D**itch negative people, influences and environments from your life.
- **E**ach day is a gift – never take it for granted.
- **F**ollow up on your action points – the fortune is always in the follow up!
- **G**et clear on what you want to do in life and go for it!
- **H**ealthy habits help you to stay disciplined and achieve more in less time.
- **I**dentify and play to your 5 key strengths.
- **J**ournal regularly to help keep your mind clear and to record ideas and flashes of inspiration.
- **K**now that "this too will pass" when you encounter challenges.

- **L**isten to and trust your intuition.
- **M**ake time for the most important people in your life.
- **N**urture yourself by spending time on the things that you are passionate about.
- **O**pen your mind to possibility. Offer solutions to challenges and don't dwell on what is wrong.
- **P**ractice random acts of kindness when you can.
- **Q**uestion existing ways of doing things to keep your mind fresh. Welcome opportunities for new experiences, it contributes to a well lived life.
- **R**egularly plan, review and reflect on your progress towards the goals you have set for yourself professionally and personally.
- **S**ay NO when you want to without feeling guilty.
- **T**ake 100% responsibility for your choices and results.
- **U**plifting people, books and quotations keep your attitude positive and spirits high. Set time aside for this area regularly.
- **V**alue and be grateful for all that you have in life.
- **W**hen you feel nervous, feel the fear and do it anyway!
- **X** factor mindsets help people to accomplish their goals. Keep your thoughts positive and optimistic.
- **Z**en like focus gets things done and helps you to complete what you start.

**Reflection time:**

Pause for a few moments and reflect on the following question:

Is there anything on the list that you need to focus more attention on this year?

## 27. Facing and overcoming fear

**"Thinking will not overcome fear but action will."**
**W.Clement Stone.**

As I mentioned in chapter 22 fear is one of the biggest interferences (obstacles) to people fulfilling their potential and that we are born with just two fears (noise and falling down).

The effect of fear on results and people's lives forms part of the coaching discussions that I have with a fair proportion of clients at some stage. It can be when I'm working with a leader of a blue chip company, a sales director, someone new to management, an individual looking to start their own business or change jobs. When people are going through or contemplating some form of change in their life, it can cause fears to crop up. Often people don't realise the impact that fear is having on them and how it's holding them back until they start talking about their goals or challenges. It's normally an unconscious behaviour.

It appears that we're all afraid of something whether it's spiders, flying, speaking in public or walking into a roomful of strangers. The philosopher Bertrand Russell said "Fear is the main source of superstition and one of the main sources of cruelty. To conquer fear is the beginning of wisdom." Fear is a very small word but can have a massive impact on someone's life and performance. It can be a powerful and paralysing force.

A summary of the fears that are most frequently referred to by clients is covered in the next couple of pages.

**The fear of failure**

Many people won't attempt something unless they can be confident that it will work successfully. Unfortunately life doesn't come with guarantees. Disappointment, setbacks and mistakes are a normal part of life and can provide rich learnings. This fear can contribute to some people procrastinating on decisions and taking action.

**The fear of rejection**

Sometimes people don't ask a question or ask for help as they don't want to be rejected. It can prevent people asking for a pay rise, a promotion or a date. Sales people don't always ask to close a sale for fear of being knocked back. It's a fear for some people when they start their own business and have to start selling themselves rather than someone else's products.

**The fear of the unknown**

We are creatures of habit and this can stop us from trying something new and different. It can mean some people stay stuck in a rut or a situation that isn't serving their best interests. The truth is life is unknown and all that is certain is the present moment, so that's good motivation to embrace opportunity and enjoy now.

**The fear of change**

The world is changing at a rapid rate fuelled by the advancement of technology. Despite this evolution, many people still fear and resist change and can become quite rigid in their approach and as a result miss opportunities.

**The fear of being judged**

Some people shy away from voicing an opinion, attending social situations or delivering presentations as they worry that they will be judged negatively by others. This can mean that they miss out on chances to advance their career, develop connections and relationships.

Facing our fears is a challenge but when we successfully do so it boasts our self-esteem. Stepping out of our comfort zone isn't easy but ultimately leads us to personal fulfilment. Our success from initial steps provides us with the courage to persevere.

There may be changes that you'd like to make in your life. You may dream of a new career, starting a business, writing a book, taking up a new hobby, doing some personal development or tackling something that holds you back. If you do, a good starting point is to be honest with yourself and clarify if a fear is stopping you implementing some changes and needs addressing.

If there's a fear you would like to overcome, getting some external help or friend's support is a good way to start the ball rolling. It provides an accountability mechanism and is a source of encouragement and external input that we all need sometimes.

**Reflection time:**

Pause for a few moments and reflect on the following questions:

Is there a fear that is holding you back? What small steps will you commit to in order to conquer the grip that it has on you?

## 28. What would you like to attract into your life?

> *"Within you right now is the power to do things you never dreamed possible. This power becomes available to you just as soon as you can change your beliefs."*
> **Dr. Maxwell Maltz.**

Earlier in the book I talked about the power of visualisation and I'm happy to include another example of how someone used visualisation to help them fulfil a dream.

I saw the actor Jim Carrey being interviewed on the Graham Norton Show and it was a very interesting discussion and insight into how Carrey used visualisation. In his career, Carrey has received four Golden Globe Award nominations, winning two. He is well known for his highly energetic slapstick performances and has been described as one of the biggest movie stars in Hollywood. Carrey started out as a stand-up comedian and received massive support and encouragement from his father to develop his career.

He said to Graham Norton that he's a big believer in visualisation and enjoys manifesting things into his life. He talked about life before his movie career took off in 1994. That year, he starred in several big name movies – Ace Ventura: Pet Detective, Dumb and Dumber and The Mask.

He explained that for four years in the lead up to landing roles in those movies, he has visualised being a successful actor. As part of the visualisation he had written a cheque for $10m made payable to himself for acting services rendered. The cheque was dated November 23rd 1995 (Thanksgiving Day). What is incredible is that he received a cheque for $10m six months before the due date on the cheque for his part in movies! He gave the cheque to his dad to thank him for the part he had played in helping him fulfil his dreams.

Jim mentioned that he learned the visualisation technique from an Irish Teacher he had at school. The teacher had told him that he prayed and asked for what he wanted and when doing so promised something in return. He said that he got whatever he wanted!

Carrey said that he tried it out when he was a child and asked for a bike. Two weeks later he came home and his parents said that he had won a Mustang Bike with chopper handlebars in a raffle. What was amusing was that he hadn't entered the raffle himself. A friend had gone into a sports goods shop and put Jim Carrey's name on a ticket (as well as his own) and hadn't told him. It was a real surprise when he won the bike.

The Jim Carrey story is an illustration of the law of attraction in action. Much has been written over the years about the Law of Attraction. I mentioned earlier in the book that Napoleon Hill wrote a book called "Think and Grow Rich" in the 1930's. Hill had been inspired to write the book after the industrialist Andrew Carnegie had disclosed his formula for personal achievement. He went on to interview 500 successful people and he found that that they had a common trait, which was the power to visualise! He famously said "Whatever the mind can conceive and believe, it can achieve."

Rhonda Byrne produced a movie and wrote a book on the topic called "The Secret" which became a best seller across the world. Esther and Jerry Hicks had written extensively on the topic some years prior to The Secret being released. Their books include "The Law of Attraction" and "Ask and It Is Given."

A book that I enjoyed reading on the subject is called "Law of Attraction, The Secret Behind The Secret" by Michael Losier. It's practical, provides some theory and is a bit of a "how to" guide.

Many people who teach the Law of Attraction discuss the vital role that being clear about what you want to attract plays and the need to believe wholeheartedly that it's possible and will happen! Many teachers suggest acting as if what you want has happened and say that you need to ask, believe and receive.

Why not give it a try? What have you got to lose? Remember to be careful for what you wish for as your dream may just come true!

**Reflection time:**

Pause for a few moments and reflect on the following question:

What would you like to attract into your life?

## 29. Never give up

**"Three grand essentials to happiness in life are something to do, something to love and something to hope for."
Joseph Addison.**

In 2015 Eddie Redmayne won the best actor category at the annual Oscars ceremony for his portrayal of Professor Stephen Hawking in the film "The Theory of Everything."

The film is an adaptation of the book - Travelling to Infinity: My Life with Stephen by Jane Wilde Hawking. It deals with her relationship with her ex-husband, his diagnosis of motor neuron disease and his success in physics. There were certain life lessons that I drew from the film which I share below:

- **Live for today and live in the present moment.** None of us know what is around the corner. Stephen Hawking was in his early twenties when he was diagnosed with Motor Neurone Disease.
- **Don't believe everything you are told.** Hawking was told he had just 2 years to live when he was diagnosed with the disease in the 1960's. He was 74 in January 2016!
- **Physical disability doesn't have to be an obstacle to achieving great things.** Hawking has achieved success with works of popular science in which he discusses his own theories and cosmology in general.
- **Don't be afraid or too proud to ask for help.** The Hawkings struggled to cope as Stephen refused outside help. This changed when Jane told Stephen about her spiralling depression. Then he said he'd understand if she needed help.

- **Never give up on your dreams and goals.** In the film Hawking said "There should be no boundaries to human endeavour. We are all different. However bad life may seem, there is always something you can do, and succeed at. While there's life, there is hope."

The story of Victor Frankl is another example of someone who showed great resilience in the face of difficulty. He was an Austrian neurologist and psychiatrist as well as a Holocaust survivor. His best-selling book, "Man's Search for Meaning" details his experiences as a concentration camp inmate which led him to discover the importance of finding meaning in all forms of existence.

The book chronicles how Frankl found meaning in the midst of extreme suffering he experienced in the harsh conditions of the Nazi concentration camp. This included a detailed account of when he was made to walk through difficult terrain in icy cold weather along with other inmates.

As they tired and struggled with the conditions, the accompanying guards kept shouting at them and driving them on with the butts of their rifles. Experiences such as this made him think of his wife and hoping that she was receiving better treatment in her camp.

He said that it helped him realise the importance of love. He said that he understood for the first time in his life the truth proclaimed as the final wisdom by so many thinkers. This truth was that love is the ultimate and the highest goal to which Man can aspire. He said that he grasped the meaning of the greatest secret that human poetry and human thought and belief have to impart: The salvation of Man is through love and in love.

He understood how someone who has nothing left in this world may still experience bliss, albeit for a brief moment, in the contemplation of his beloved.

I believe that stories such as Stephen Hawking's and Victor Frankel's are perfect illustrations of the strength of the human spirit and how in the face of great adversity people find the courage to persevere and endure suffering. They can serve as an inspiration to us all.

**Reflection time:**

Pause for a few moments and reflect on the following questions:

Who do you know that has shown great perseverance in the face of difficulty?

What lessons has their determination taught you?

## 30. Multi-tasking makes your brain smaller

*"Concentrate all your thoughts upon the work at hand. The sun's rays do not burn until brought to a focus."*
**Alexander Graham Bell.**

Whilst researching techniques to effectively manage time and be more focused, I came across some interesting research and information on multi-tasking.

According to an article written by the Daily Mail's Fiona Macrae and Mail on-line's Ellie Zolfagharifard multi-tasking shrinks the brain. A study found that people who frequently used several types of technology at the same time had less grey matter in a key part of the brain. Grey matter is the part of the brain that processes information.

University of Sussex researchers said: "Simultaneously using mobile phones, laptops and other media devices could be changing the structure of our brains."

Worryingly, the part of the brain that shrinks is involved in processing emotion. The finding follows research which has linked multi-tasking with a shortened attention span, depression, anxiety and lower grades at school.

The researchers began by asking healthy men and women how often they divided their attention between different types of technology. This could mean sending a text message while listening to music and checking email, or speaking on the phone while watching TV and surfing the web. The volunteers were then given brain scans which showed they had less grey matter in a region called the anterior cingulate cortex (ACC).

The findings held even when differences in personality were taken into account.

The study, published in the journal Plos one is the first to make a link between multi-tasking and the structure of the brain. Researcher Kep Kee Loh said: "Media multi-tasking is becoming more prevalent in our lives today and there is increasing concern about its impact on our cognition and social-emotional well-being."

He added that more research is needed to prove that multi-tasking shrinks the brain. This is because it's also possible that people with less grey matter in the ACC are more drawn to using lots of gadgets simultaneously. Scientists have previously demonstrated brain structure can be altered on prolonged exposure to novel environments and experience. Experts have also warned of the harmful impact technology can have on our memory and attention span.

The University of California team commissioned a survey of more than 18,000 people aged between 18 and 99 and found 20 per cent had problems with memory. Researchers were taken aback by the 14 per cent of 18 to 39-year-olds who also worried about their memories. Multi-tasking with gadgets may shorten attention span, making it harder to focus and form memories, the researchers said, adding that youngsters may be particularly affected by stress.

If you would like to improve focus or concentration here are a few suggestions:

- **Focus on one task at a time.** Complete things before you move onto something else. A short break to deal with

emails, send texts or take quick phone calls makes it very hard to focus. Some research suggests it takes 15 minutes after a distraction to completely focus.
- **Shut out distractions,** whilst working on those tasks that require lots of focus (such as devising a report or preparing budgets). This can include closing e mail/chat boxes, turning off notifications of incoming mail/messages on social media. If possible shut yourself away in an office or work from home to increase focus.
- **Compartmentalise.** Set specific time aside to deal with worries and things that are playing on your mind. It isn't easy to concentrate on a task if you are constantly worrying about other things. Make a note of things that are causing you concern. Park them and return to them when you have completed the task at hand.
- **Take short breaks.** It's demanding and our minds aren't really able to cope with focus with intensity for eight hours each day. It's good to chunk up your time into one hour segments and take 5/10 minute breaks in between tasks and meetings. This gives the brain a rest before you refocus.

**Reflection time:**

Pause for a few moments and reflect on the following questions:

What action do you need to take to improve your level of focus and concentration levels?

What one step could you take to increase your personal effectiveness?

### 31. Listening is the best form of influence

*"Too often we underestimate the power of a touch, a smile, a kind word, a listening ear, an honest compliment, or the smallest act of caring, all of which have the potential to turn a life around." Leo Buscaglia.*

I've mentioned previously that we live in an information rich and time poor world. This environment can lead to people feeling overwhelmed and having to multi-task.

One of the most powerful and important lessons, I learnt early in my career concerned listening and how it improved your influencing skills. When I finished full time education, the company I joined included me on their management development programme. As part of the programme it was suggested that we read a book by Dale Carnegie called "How to Win Friends and Influence People." It was the first personal development book that I read.

The powerful lesson and key message I took from the book was that an easy way to be a good conversationalist was to be a great listener and encourage others to talk about themselves. In following this approach you help people to feel heard, valued and special. This increases your influence authentically.

Dale Carnegie's book quotes a journalist called Isaac F Marcosson, who interviewed hundreds of celebrities. It was his view that many people fail to make a favourable impression and diminish their influence because they don't listen attentively. He said "They have been so much concerned with what they are going to say next they don't keep their ears open. Very important people have told me that they prefer good listeners to talkers, but the ability to listen seems rarer than almost any other good trait."

How to Win Friends and Influence People was first published in 1953 and I wonder if the increased number of gadgets at our disposal has further reduced our ability and capacity to listen attentively. Many people these days seem to want to talk more than they listen. As the famous quote by Zeno of Citium says "We have two ears and one mouth, so we should listen more than we say."

Being a good listener is a great way to stand out in today's busy world and is as important in our personal lives as in the world of business.

Having great listening skills doesn't come easily given the number of distractions that fill the modern world. It requires us to calm our busy minds and have a genuine desire to want to listen to others.

We have so much outside noise to filter that it's a real challenge to listen to other people. It necessitates us to make a commitment to limit the number of distractions. It may involve turning off televisions, phones, pc's/tablets and managing potential interruptions. Following these disciplines clearly shows that you care and value the person you are listening to. It also demonstrates that you have good social skills. Being a good listener takes time, practice and commitment.

When listening to another you need to give them your full attention and ensure that "you are in the room" rather than having your mind focused on something other than what the person is discussing. Although, it sounds obvious, it's imperative that you stay quiet when the other person is talking as talking over them or interrupting can suggest a lack of respect. Creating an environment with some pauses and brief periods of silence puts people at ease and gives them a chance to reflect and think.

Another way to demonstrate that you're listening effectively is through your body language and eye contact. Relaxed and open posture shows people that you are genuinely interested in what they have to say. Good eye contact is essential to show that you're actively engaged in the conversation and paying attention. Nothing shows people more that you're not really interested by breaking eye contact, looking over their shoulder and fixing your gaze elsewhere whilst they are in full flow.

Good listening also requires that you approach conversations with an open mind and intent to really engage with what the speaker is saying. A good listener has natural empathy with a genuine and authentic desire to understand what the other person is communicating.

**Reflection time:**

Pause for a few moments and reflect on the following questions:

What one thing could you do to develop your ability to listen?

What benefits will it bring you to do so?

## 32. Maintaining a positive attitude

> "Attitude is a little thing that makes a big difference."
> **Sir Winston Churchill.**

I've talked previously in the book about positive and negative people and the impact they have on our energy levels. We all have challenges sometimes and a positive attitude allows us to face into what life throws at us. It also helps us recover more quickly from negative situations.

A positive attitude was one of the key factors in the success of Thomas Edison who I mentioned earlier. He was an optimist and said "many of life's failures are people who didn't realise how close they were to success when they gave up."

Probably the most notable display of Edison's positive attitude was in the way he approached a tragedy that occurred when he was in his late sixties. The laboratory he had built, a fourteen building complex, which was greater in size than three football pitches, caught fire.

Now he loved this place. It was the base of his operations, it was where he and his staff conceived inventions, developed prototypes, manufactured products and shipped them to customers. It had become a model for modern research and manufacturing. He spent every minute he could there. He often slept there on one of the laboratory tables.

When it caught fire, he was reported as saying as he stood outside and watched it burn and his life's work go up in smoke, "Quick kids go and get your mother she'll never see another fire like this one." Most people would've been crushed by this event, but not Edison, he said, "I'm 67, but not too old to make a fresh start. I've been through a lot of things like this." He rebuilt the laboratory and he kept working for another 17 years.

Here are a few ideas and suggestions to maintain and increase your positivity levels:

1. **Defer worrying.** Put off worrying until you have a reason to worry. We can all spend lots of time locked in our heads imagining all sorts of scenarios that never actually happen. I was told that 70% of what we worry about never happens, 25% is trivia and 5 % is out of our control.
2. **Be self – disciplined.** Setting clear goals and taking daily action helps raise our esteem and confidence levels. Having daily rituals mean that we make the best use of our time. Many people resist structure for fear that it sucks the fun out of their life, when in fact it gives us the freedom to make the most of our leisure time.
3. **Appreciate all that you have in life.** Take a few minutes each day to write down 3 things that you're grateful for. It helps you focus your mind on what you have rather than what you lack. This develops an abundance mindset rather than one of scarcity. Like attracts like, this simple act will attract even more things to be grateful for into your life
4. **Hang out with positive people.** Be discerning about the company that you keep. Avoid toxic people and situations. Associate with people that have belief and faith in you and encourage you to develop and grow. Socialise with people that aim high, think positivity, genuinely care about you and make you laugh. Be that person for them too.
5. **Remember to laugh.** Nothing increases your mood and energy levels more than a good belly laugh. The news coverage can contain lots of negative and sad stories.

Regularly watch things that make you laugh. Take a break from news bulletins and newspapers from time to time. Read something funny or look at a book of humorous cartoons.

6. **Keep a journal.** If you do find that your mood dips or you're having a challenging time, write down your feelings and frustrations as this will help release any hurt, confusion or negative thoughts. It externalises what you're thinking and brings clarity, calmness and a sense of balance. It restores you to positivity.
7. **Maintain your boundaries.** Say no when you need to without feeling guilty. We all have limited time and energy and it's important we address our own needs. Saying yes, when you actually want to say no does nothing for your self-esteem and can have a negative impact on your mood.
8. **Practice self-care.** Make good health an absolute priority. If you have good health you have everything and it helps you to keep good energy levels and a positive frame of mind. Your health truly is your wealth. Aerobic exercise releases endorphins and helps to reduce body tension. Get sufficient sleep and count your calories.

**Reflection time:**

Pause for a few moments and reflect on the following question:

What steps can you take to increase your positivity?

## 33. How productive are your meetings?

> *"Always go into meetings or negotiations with a positive attitude. Tell yourself you're going to make this the best deal for all parties."* Natalie Massenet.

Whilst it would be foolish to condemn all meetings as a waste of time, they do hold great potential for time wasting. A major source of frustration for many of my corporate coaching clients is the amount of time they have to spend in meetings each week. It seems the larger the company; the more unproductive meetings that take place.

According to a study in 2012 carried out by Opinion Matters on behalf of Epson, the average worker wastes 2 hours and thirty nine minutes in meetings each week, which equates to £26 billion of lost income to the UK economy. One reason that employees cite for this is that some meetings are too long and their attention span gets stretched to the limit leading to information failing to go in after a certain point.

Apparently it takes the average employee just 11 minutes to lose focus and not pay attention to what's being discussed. Distractions such as colleagues arriving late and the use of laptops, smartphones and tablets by others is a reason why 68% of respondents said they become distracted and lose focus.

There are some common complaints clients tell me about the meetings that they attend. These include having to be at meetings where their attendance isn't always required but is expected out of habit. Another issue that's near the top of their list of irritants is the time that's wasted by going around in circles, discussing the same issues week in week out without coming up with solutions. Others mention that the meetings they attend rarely start and finish on time and are too long. They also get frustrated by the need for recaps for people who arrive late.

It appears that many meetings aren't chaired very well, don't have a clear agenda or objectives and rarely come up with clear action points. Given how busy life is and how resources are so stretched in many organisations, it makes sense to regularly review the amount of time that's spent in meetings and ensure that they are a productive use of time.

It may be helpful to consider if there are more efficient ways of doing things. For instance, are there alternative or better ways of communicating and sharing information? This may include the use of technology to avoid travelling time and expense. Is it possible for people to come to you for particular meetings to save on your travel time?

You can encourage all the teams you are involved with to adopt some best practices:-

- Ensure all meetings have a clear purpose and objectives, which are clearly communicated and understood by everyone in attendance.
- A focused agenda with some time slots allocated for each agenda item ensures that meetings are more productive and stick to allocated time.
- Consider reducing the length of meetings from 60 minute slots to 45 minutes.
- Stop doing recaps for late arrivals or holding/attending meetings with no agenda and clear objectives.

- Consider rotating the role of meeting chairperson, so junior members of the team get the chance to develop and experience what it's like to keep the meeting focused and productive. It also keeps the meetings fresh and helps people to grow and develop new skills.

I suggest to clients that together with their colleagues they regularly review the effectiveness of meetings. They can do this by answering and rating the following questions on a scale of 1-10 (10 being high):-

- How clear were the objectives?
- How focused was the agenda/purpose of the meeting?
- How well did the group plan?
- How well did the group manage time and stick to agreed timings?
- How well were priorities set?
- How well was everybody involved and included in discussions?
- How well was conflict and disagreement handled?
- How much responsibility did everyone take for the successful running of the meeting?
- How clear were the agreed action points?

There are some supplementary questions detailed below that can also be asked to help improve the effectiveness of meetings:

- What ideas do you have to make these meetings more productive and effective? What alternative ways could we communicate and share information with each other?
- Was your attendance at the meeting absolutely necessary?

**Reflection time:**

Pause for a few moments and consider the meetings that you attend and reflect on the following questions:

What steps can you take to make your meetings more effective and focused?

Is there an opportunity for you to save some time by attending fewer meetings or reducing the length of them?

## 34. Negative experiences can have positive outcomes

> "Every problem has a gift for you in its hands."
> **Richard Bach.**

On occasions things don't turn out the way we envisaged and we feel disappointed. Sometimes, as time goes by we come to realise that the negative experience was actually a springboard to something more positive. The following story is a great example of a negative experience that had a positive outcome. It was featured in a book called the Flipside by Adam Jackson.

On the evening of September 22 1963, four young men set off in a car from Majadahonda to Madrid in Spain. The four were all good friends enjoying the night out, but it was to be a journey they would never forget.

Julio was one of the four men in the car that night. His dream was to become a professional football player and play for the team he had loved as a boy, Real Madrid. He had nurtured his dream and pursued it from his earliest years and that dream was just beginning to be realized. He had immense talent and emerged as something of a prodigy.

Real Madrid had signed Julio as a goalkeeper and he was widely tipped to be the future goalkeeper for the Spanish national team. Life couldn't have been better for Julio; his star was on the rise, until the evening he stepped into the car with his friends. As fate would have it, his dream would end that night.

At around 2.00 a.m. the car that Julio and his friends were travelling in was involved in a serious accident. Julio awoke in Madrid's Eloy Gonzalo Hospital to discover that he was semi-paralysed. The doctors informed him that he would need to be confined to a bed for eighteen months in order to give his spinal injuries time to heal. Even then, the prognosis wasn't good. They thought it would be unlikely that Julio would ever walk again. But there was one thing that wasn't in doubt. His football career was over.

At night, during those eighteen months in hospital Julio would listen to the radio and write poems – sad, reflective, romantic verses that questioned man's fate and the meaning of life. On reading the poems that Julio had written, one of the young male nurses that was taking care of him, a man called Eladio Magdaleno, gave Julio a guitar and suggested he turned the poems into songs.

Singing began as a distraction for Julio, a way of forgetting happier times spent as an athlete. But, as time went on, the singing became more of a passion than a distraction. He scribbled numbers on the guitar to learn the basic chords. Every week, more and more would appear and within a short time he was creating melodies for his poems.

When the eighteen months had passed and Julio had recovered from his injuries, he decided to return to Murcia University to resume his studies. Later, he travelled to England to improve his English. Occasionally, at weekends he would sing in the Airport Pub covering songs that were popular at that time from the likes of Tom Jones, Engelbert Humperdinck and The Beatles

When Julio returned home to Spain, he looked for a singer to perform his songs. He took his first song to a recording studio in Madrid and asked if they could recommend a singer. The manager, looking at Julio and listening to him perform the song, was confused. Why would a man like Julio need someone to sing his songs? Julio was a strikingly handsome man with jet-black hair; large brown eyes, a smooth, tanned complexion and a smile that could make most women go weak at the knees. He also had a distinctive singing voice that was pitch-perfect. "Why don't you just perform it yourself?" the manager asked. Julio answered "because I am not a singer!"

Eventually, Julio took the manager's advice and entered one of his songs in a Spanish music contest. On 17 July 1968, just under 5 years after the accident that nearly destroyed his life, he won first prize at the Fiesta de Benidorm with the song "La Vida Sigue Iqual" (Life goes on the same) and soon after, he was offered a contract with Columbia Records.

Chances are, you will have heard Julio singing or maybe you own one of his albums. For the man who had lost his boyhood dreams in that tragic car accident went on to become the biggest selling recording artist in the history of Latin American music and a household name. His name is Julio Iglesias and father of the pop star Enrique Iglesias.

**Reflection time:**

Pause for a few moments and reflect on the following question:

What would you do if you knew things would work out well?

## 35. Quality is a habit

**"Be a yardstick of quality. Some people aren't used to an environment where excellence is expected." Steve Jobs.**

Steve Jobs was an American information technology entrepreneur and inventor who prior to his death in October 2011 was the co-founder, chairman and chief executive officer of Apple Inc. He helped to build Apple into the world's most valuable company. Shortly after his death, Job's official biographer, Walter Issacson, described him as the "creative entrepreneur" whose passion for perfection and ferocious drive revolutionized six industries: personal computers, animated movies, music, phones, tablet computing and digital publishing.

Apple is known for the quality of its products and this is an ethos that is deeply entrenched in the company's culture. For instance, their current CEO, Tim Cook, when outlining the company's business philosophy said "we don't settle for anything less than excellence in every group in the company."

Steve Jobs was said to be obsessed with the way things were crafted and the quality of the unseen parts. He wasn't just content to meet specifications; he frequently went above and beyond to ensure that the products he had a hand in were made in the best way possible. Much has been written about Jobs perfectionism, attention to detail and the way he drove his people.

Jobs and Apple produced a string of very successful quality products over the years greater than any other modern day innovation company. These included: iMac, iPod, iPod Nano, iTunes Store, Apple Stores, MacBook, iPhone, iPad, App Stores, OS X Lion – not to mention every Pixar film.

Walter Isaacson suggests in the Steve Jobs biography that the likely source of this focus on craftsmanship was Jobs adoptive father, Paul Jobs. He was a mechanic, good with his hands and his work focused mainly on cars.

"I thought my dad's sense of design was pretty good," Jobs told Isaacson, "because he knew how to build anything. If we needed a cabinet, he would build it. When he built our fence, he gave me a hammer so I could work with him." His uncompromising attitude towards quality originates from a very specific moment in his childhood about painting a garden fence.

Fifty years after the fence was constructed, Jobs showed it to Isaacson, still standing and recalled the lesson his father taught him he would never forget. Touching the boards of the inside of the fence, he said that "he loved doing things right. He even cared about the look of the unseen parts."

As a curious child Steve wondered why his father would paint the parts of the fence that you couldn't see as you would use less paint if you skipped those parts and also get the job done quicker. His father told him that a great craftsman cares about doing a great job and if you compromise with the quality in any part of a quality product, even in a hidden place, then you don't have a quality product.

Paul Jobs said that it was important for him to know he had done the best that he could. Whilst others wouldn't be able to see the hidden parts of the fence, he would know that the fence hadn't been painted inside and therefore couldn't consider it to be a quality job.

He said that his father refused to use poor wood for the back of cabinets, or to build a fence that wasn't constructed as well on the back side as it was the front. Jobs likened it to using a piece of plywood on the back of a beautiful chest of drawers. "For you to sleep well at night, the aesthetic, the quality, has to be carried all the way through."

This is a good rule of thumb to remember. If you want to know whether you are looking at the work of a merely good craftsman or that of a great craftsman, simply look at the hidden parts and see if those are done properly as well. Jobs would recall the lessons taught by his father about the attention worth paying, even to the things unseen, throughout his career and life and users of Apple products often reaped the rewards.

**Reflection time:**

Pause for a few moments and reflect on the projects and work that you're involved with and consider the following questions:

Are there some tweaks or changes that you can make to improve the quality of your output?

If you lead or manage a team, is there anything that you can do to inspire your people to improve the quality of your products and service?

## 36. Courage is a great quality

> **"Courage is the most important of all the virtues, because without courage you can't practice any other virtue consistently. You can practice any virtue erratically, but nothing consistently without courage." Maya Angelou.**

A human quality that always impresses and inspires me is courage which is defined by the Oxford dictionary "as the ability to disregard fear, to be brave and act on one's beliefs." Aristotle called courage the first virtue, because it makes all of the other virtues possible.

I enjoy reading stories about how people stood up for what they believed in despite opposition. There are countless tales from history of people who made significant personal sacrifice, displayed incredible conviction and made a personal stand against injustice. In showing great fortitude and battling against the odds they helped to create more freedom and rights for millions of people to enjoy and bring about justice.

In the late 19th and early 20th century, suffragettes were members of women's organisations in the UK which advocated the right for women to vote in public elections. The term "suffragette" is particularly associated with activists in the British WSPU, led by Emmeline and Christabel Pankhurst. Many of them were imprisoned for their actions and staged hunger strikes.

It's hard to believe that less than 100 years ago women weren't able to vote in elections. Whilst I don't condone some of their tactics, their personal actions and courage did lead to significant and valid change in the United Kingdom.

It wasn't until the Equal Franchise Act of 1928 that women over 21 were able to vote and women finally achieved the same voting rights as men. The laws at the time also disadvantaged men, as only men who had been resident in the country for 12 months prior to a general election were entitled to vote. This meant that those returning from fighting in World War One were unable to vote in elections!

December 2015 saw the 60th anniversary of a very brave act by a lady called Rosa Parks from Montgomery, Alabama, USA. Her courage led to improved human rights for black people in America

It's difficult to comprehend that 60 years ago there were segregation laws in place in the USA. One consequence of the law was that black Americans had to vacate their seats on buses if there were white passengers left standing.

Rosa Parks was tired after a day's work. She was employed as a seamstress, doing repairs on men's clothing at a department store called Montgomery Fair. She was suffering from aches and pains in her shoulders, back and neck.

Therefore, on that day (December 1st 1955) she made a stand and refused to give up her seat to a white person. She was arrested for violating segregation laws and at a subsequent court appearance was fined $10. This was not the first time she had acted in this way, as she had refused to give up her seat in 1943.

Mrs Parks was also a youth leader of the local branch of NAACP who worked for the advancement of rights for black people. Along with her husband Raymond, she worked for years to improve the lot of black Americans in the southern

United States where rigid segregation laws had been in force since the end of the Civil War in 1865. In protest at the fine levied on Mrs Parks, nearly all Montgomery's 40,000 black citizens took part in the bus boycott, which lasted for 381 days. Martin Luther King had been one of those that had addressed a crowd at Holt Street Baptist Church in support of the boycott.

The NAACP decided to use her case as a test against city and state segregation laws. Eventually the US Supreme court upheld the decision of a lower court to end segregation on Alabama's buses. It all started with Rosa Parks being courageous and seeking to initiate change.

Courage tends to be contagious. When someone stands up for what they believe to be right, it encourages and inspires others to find some strength. We all need to find courage sometimes. Maybe it's to overcome a fear that we have, to try a new approach to an old challenge, to step outside our comfort zone or take up a new hobby.

When we want to develop a new skill or overcome a habit that is inhibiting our growth and fulfilment of our potential it requires us to step into the unknown and be courageous. In order for us to speak our truth, to confront unacceptable behaviour or to ask for what we want, it requires some degree of courage on our part.

**Reflection time:**

Pause for a few moments and reflect on the following question:

What step would you take today if you were brave?

## 37. Taking time to express appreciation

**"Gratitude can transform common days into thanksgivings, turn routine jobs into joy, and change ordinary opportunities into blessings." William Arthur Ward.**

May 8th 2015 was the anniversary of VE Day (Victory in Europe Day), marking 70 years since the end of the Second World War in Europe. On that day I reflected on how much suffering this and other wars had brought to many people and the continued debt of gratitude we owe to those people who put their lives on the line to protect our democracy and freedom.

A story that came to mind was about Captain Charles Plumb and the war that the USA fought in Vietnam. It's a great reminder about the importance of taking more time to express appreciation.

Captain Plumb graduated from the Naval Academy at Annapolis. After graduating, Plumb completed Navy Flight Training and reported to Miramar Naval Air Station in San Diego where he flew the first adversarial flights in the development of what would be called The Navy Fighter Weapons School, currently known as "TOP GUN". He went on to fly the F-4 Phantom jet on 74 successful combat missions over Vietnam. On his 75th mission, with only five days before he was to return home, Plumb was shot down, captured, tortured, and imprisoned in an 8 foot x 8 foot cell. He spent the next 2,103 days as a Prisoner Of War in communist war prisons.

During his nearly six years of captivity, Charlie Plumb distinguished himself among his fellow prisoners as a professional in underground communications and served for two of those years as the Chaplain in his camp. He received many military honours.

Here is his true story called "Packing Parachutes"

"Recently, I was sitting in a restaurant in Kansas City. A man about two tables away kept looking at me. I didn't recognize him. A few minutes into our meal he stood up and walked over to my table, looked down at me, pointed his finger in my face and said, "You're Captain Plumb."

I looked up and I said, "Yes sir, I'm Captain Plumb."

He said, "You flew jet fighters in Vietnam. You were on the aircraft carrier Kitty Hawk. You were shot down and parachuted into enemy hands and spent six years as a prisoner of war." I said, "How in the world did you know all that?"

He replied, "Because, I packed your parachute." I was speechless. I staggered to my feet and held out a very grateful hand of thanks. This guy came up with just the proper words. He grabbed my hand; he pumped my arm and said, "I guess it worked."

"Yes sir, indeed it did", I said, "and I must tell you I've said a lot of prayers of thanks for your nimble fingers, but I never thought I'd have the opportunity to express my gratitude in person."

He said, "Were all the panels there?"

"Well sir, I must shoot straight with you," I said, "of the eighteen panels that were supposed to be in that parachute, I had fifteen good ones. Three were torn, but it wasn't your fault, it was mine. I jumped out of that jet fighter at a high rate of speed, close to the ground. That's what tore the panels in the chute. It wasn't the way you packed it."

"Let me ask you a question," I said, "do you keep track of all the parachutes you pack?" "No" he responded, "it's enough gratification for me just to know that I've served."

I didn't get much sleep that night. I kept thinking about that man. I kept wondering what he might have looked like in a Navy uniform – a Dixie cup hat, a bib in the back and bell bottom trousers. I wondered how many times I might have passed him on board the Kitty Hawk. I wondered how many times I might have seen him and not even said "good morning", "how are you", or anything because, you see, I was a fighter pilot and he was just a sailor. How many hours did he spend on that long wooden table in the bowels of that ship weaving the shrouds and folding the silks of those chutes? I could not have cared less, until one day my parachute came along and he packed it for me."

It occurred to me that in today's busy world, it's not always easy to consistently translate our thoughts of appreciation into words and acts of gratitude. We can fail to show true appreciation to those that help, support and encourage us.

**Reflection time:**

Pause for a few moments and reflect on the following question:

Who do you need to show some appreciation to for the help, support and encouragement they provide to you?

## 38. Laughter is the best medicine

**"A day without laughter is a day wasted." Charlie Chaplin.**

One of the sayings that I remember from my childhood is "laughter is the best medicine." I'd assumed that it was a biblical quote but it doesn't appear in the bible. However, it probably originates from a quote in Proverbs: "A joyful heart is good medicine but a broken spirit dries up the bones."

Whilst researching the benefits of laughter I came across an interesting story about Norman Cousins who was an American political journalist, author, professor and world peace advocate who died in 1990 aged 75. Remarkably, Cousins was diagnosed in 1964 as having a serious disease and was told that his chances for survival were one in five hundred and that he had just months to live.

But Cousins had a strong will to live, so he decided to assume most of the responsibility for his own healing. Having been told that he had little chance of surviving, he developed a recovery programme. It included big doses of Vitamin C, along with a positive attitude and laughter induced by Marx Brothers films and anything else that he could get his hands on to make him laugh. Cousins developed a systematic programme for getting daily doses of hearty laughter.

He said "I made the joyous discovery that ten minutes of genuine belly laughter had an anaesthetic effect and would give me at least two hours of pain-free sleep." It's remarkable that he was able to laugh having been told he had an irreversible disease and didn't have long to live. He wrote of his healing experiences in "Anatomy of an illness."

Medical tests done since then have established that there's a physiological basis for the theory that laughter is good medicine.

After his remarkable recovery, Cousins continued to study the effects of positive emotions on the human system. Eventually, he joined the medical faculty at the UCLA Medical School, a rare appointment for a person without a medical degree.

Cousins was one of the pioneers in linking laughter to healing. Since his initial explorations, his research has been duplicated by many both in and out of the medical profession. These include Dr Bernie Siegel and Dr Patch Adams. Both have written extensively about the power of humour and hope in the healing process. A film called Patch Adams about Dr Adams work is worth watching. It is heart-warming, funny and based on scientific evidence.

Laughter Yoga is gaining in popularity worldwide. It was made popular as an exercise routine developed by Indian Physician Madan Kataria. It's a practice that involves prolonged voluntary laughter and is based on the belief that voluntary laughter provides the same physiological and psychological benefits as spontaneous laughter. It's done in groups and laughter is easily stimulated and sustained with eye contact, exercises and playfulness amongst the participants.

Sessions start with gentle warm-up techniques which include stretching, chanting, clapping and body movement. These help break down inhibitions. Breathing exercises help prepare the lungs for laughter, followed by a series of laughter exercises.

During my research, I found the following information from the Mayo Clinic about the short and long term benefits of laughter:-

**Some of the short-term benefits that laughter can bring:**

- Enhances intake of oxygen-rich air, stimulates your heart, lungs and muscles and increases the endorphins that are released by your brain.
- Activate and relieve your stress response and lead to a good relaxed feeling.
- Soothe tension, stimulate circulation and aid muscle relaxation.

**Some of the long-term benefits that laughter may bring:**

- Pain relief by causing the body to produce its own natural painkillers. Laughter may also break the pain-spasm cycle common to some muscle disorders.
- Increase personal satisfaction and can make it easier to cope with difficult situations as it helps you to connect with other people.
- Improve your mood, it can reduce depression and anxiety and increase happiness.

**Reflection time:**

Pause for a few moments and reflect on the following question:

What steps can you take to introduce more laughter into your life?

### 39. The importance of self-belief on results

> "You have to believe in yourself! Have faith in your abilities! Without a humble but reasonable confidence in your own powers you cannot be successful or happy."
> **Norman Vincent Peale.**

Sport has always been a passion of mine whether as part of a team or as a spectator. One of the things that I've observed over the years is the massive role that self-belief has on individual or team performance levels and results. It's a subject that fascinates me including the importance of people creating the right mental state in order for them to perform at their best. For a long time I've believed that sports people and athletes simply don't perform at their best without self- belief and confidence.

The same principle applies in business and life in general. I'm sure you've experienced periods where you have felt good and had great belief in yourself or your team, your capabilities and prospects. At times like these things seem to flow, performance levels get better as if by magic and results are generated with ease.

However, it may be that when you have suffered a set-back or disappointment, it can have a detrimental impact on your self-belief. When this happens the tasks that you have to perform seem to take more effort. Things can feel a bit laboured and results don't flow with the same grace and ease. In periods like this it can feel like good fortune has temporarily deserted you.

If you're going to be successful in accomplishing a particular goal or dream, it's important that you believe that you can achieve it and make it happen. You may have a dream of starting your own business, taking up a new hobby or learning to drive. Maybe you have started a new job or at the start of the year you were allocated goals and objectives to achieve at work.

Whatever your own particular goal is you have to believe that you're properly equipped to succeed and that you have the right capabilities and skills. You may refer to self-belief as self-confidence or self-esteem. Whatever your description you have to believe in yourself and that you have what it takes to create your desired results.

It's essential that you believe that you have the requisite resources and mental strength to accomplish what you set out to do. I have detailed below some thoughts and tips on how self-belief can be developed:

**Make a list of your key accomplishments and things that you have achieved in life that you are proud of.** You can refer to this list often to keep your self-belief levels high. It's particularly important to do this when you suffer a setback or disappointment. This simple act will help you to restore some balance in your perspective and enable you to bounce back quicker.

**Get clear on your key talents and strengths.** What are the skills and abilities that you contribute to life and teams that you are part of professionally and/or personally? As I've mentioned previously, many people are able to clearly outline what they are not good at or what they need to improve. Very few can clearly articulate their strengths and the value that they bring to life.

**Delete "I can't" from your vocabulary.** When you catch yourself saying I can't do this because you are too old, not experienced enough or whatever is your own negative belief, change your thought pattern. I suggest that instead of saying "I can't" Start saying "I can do this." Ask yourself what support, resources or help you need in order that you can achieve your goals.

**Set goals that are realistic.** There's no point having goals that are far too stretching or unrealistic. When we fail to meet them our belief levels plummet. Setting and meeting goals helps to grow self-belief. Once you've met your target, you're able to make the next goal a bit more stretching.

**Quit the comparison game.** Stop comparing your life and results to others as you will never find someone at exactly the same point in life as yourself! Redirect the energy that you use on comparing yourself to others on setting clear goals and targets for your life. Then focus your attention and efforts on achieving these and reviewing your progress.

**Reflection time:**

Pause for a few moments and reflect on the following questions:

On a scale of 0-10(with 10 being high) what score would you give yourself for your level of self-belief at present?

If you would like to increase your personal score, what action steps can you take to improve the score?

### 40. Ask questions and avoid making assumptions

> **"Appreciation is a wonderful thing: It makes what is excellent in others belong to us as well." Voltaire.**

Clear communication and getting clarity is always better than making assumptions. As the old phrase says "to assume is to make an ass of you and me!" When we don't have a full understanding of a situation we can fill in the gaps by making up a story in our minds. This helps us to make sense of people and situations. However, this approach is fraught with danger as we can form false opinions.

Instead of making assumptions, an alternative strategy may be to get better at asking questions to bring increased clarity. Asking effective questions helps to build our understanding of situations and get to the core of issues. Posing questions from a position of natural curiosity with a genuine intent to understand enables us to develop a greater empathy for people. It helps to strengthen and deepen relationships. It can save energy as we don't have to use our brains to create stories.

When we ask questions we may uncover opinions and views that are different to our own. It may give us an answer that we weren't expecting or particularly agree with. In this case, it's worth reminding ourselves that life is all about opinions and that what's right for one person is not right for others.

Having different perspectives and viewpoints is good in reaching better and more balanced solutions. I believe that diversity of views and ideas is something to be encouraged.

Time spent having a greater tolerance of people who have different opinions to our own helps build our capacity to influence.

It's impossible for us to be experts in all areas of life. It's helpful to seek the thoughts of others and for them to share their knowledge and experience. This input can be very beneficial.

We're all human, none of us are perfect or right one hundred per cent of the time. However, I'm sure you've met or know people who (in their world) are always right and argue that the colour black is in fact white!

If you come across people like that in the future and feel yourself getting irritated and frustrated by their attitude remind yourself of the following story. Hopefully it will help you to smile and reduce your stress levels.

I believe the story is a good reminder to guard against making assumptions and to ask questions to get clarity. It's called The Cookie Thief written by Valerie Cox.

**The Cookie Thief**

A woman was waiting at an airport one night. With several long hours before her flight, she bought a book and a bag of cookies. She then found a place where she could sit and do her reading.

She was engrossed in her book but noticed that the man beside her was grabbing some cookies "from the bag between." She tried to ignore the situation because she wanted to avoid making a scene.

The situation continued for some time. As she read and munched her cookies, the man was continuing to eat the cookies, too. She also continued to ignore him but she told herself, "If I wasn't so nice, I'd blacken his eye!"

Then, finally, there was only one cookie left. The man took the last cookie and broke it in half. With a smile on his face, he offered her half and ate the other. She took the other half and thought, "This guy has some nerve, and he's also rude. He didn't even show any gratitude."

Right there and then, she wanted to say something but her flight was called. She gathered all her belongings and headed for the gate, refusing to look back at the "cookie thief." She boarded the plane and continued reading her book. In the middle of the flight, she reached into her back pack and "gasped with surprise." She found her bag of cookies inside it.

"If mine are here," she said, "then the cookies we were eating were his and he tried to share them with me." It was too late to apologise. She realised that she was the rude one and the thief.

**Reflection time:**

Pause for a few moments and reflect on the following question:

Is there a situation where you are making an assumption and need to ask questions to get some clarity and develop your understanding?

## 41. The power of random acts of kindness

> "Never believe that a few caring people can't change the world. For, indeed, that's all who ever have."
> **Margaret Mead.**

One of my favourite films is "Pay it forward" the story of a 12-year-old schoolboy in Las Vegas called Trevor McKinney. He's troubled by his mother's alcoholism and fears of his abusive but absent father. However, he really engaged and got inspired by an intriguing assignment from his new social studies teacher, Mr Simonet.

The project set by the teacher is for the pupils to come up with a plan to positively change the world through direct action. On his way home from school later that day, Trevor notices a homeless man, Jerry and decides to make a difference in Jerry's life by housing and feeding him until he gets back on his feet.

Trevor then comes up with his pay it forward plan to help more people. This consists of people doing a random act of kindness for three people who must in turn each do a good deed for three others. In doing so they are creating a charitable pyramid scheme and helping to make the world a better place.

The idea catches on and spreads from city to city. It reaches the attention of national press who record an interview with Trevor. He explains his hopes for the concept but voices his concerns that people may be too afraid to change their own lives in order to make the whole world a better place.

A story from 2014 illustrates how acts of kindness can spread and make a big difference concerns an amazing young man called Stephen Sutton. The terminally ill 19 year old cancer patient from Staffordshire posted a heart-breaking farewell on his Facebook page with the message "It's a final thumbs up from me."

Stephen had raised thousands of pounds for charity by charting his illness on social media and had won the hearts of well-wishers. In his final message from his hospital bed, he said "I've done well to blag things as well as I have up till now but unfortunately, I think this is just one hurdle too far. It's a shame the end has come so suddenly. There's so many people I haven't got round to properly thank or say goodbye to, apologies for that. There were also so many exciting projects and things I didn't get to see out. If you want to carry on the fundraising please do."

The comedian Jason Manford had met Stephen on several occasions when organising and hosting the annual Teenage Cancer Trust comedy galas at the Royal Albert Hall. Jason was so moved by what Stephen had written that he directed his own army of followers on Twitter and Facebook to help make Stephen's desire to reach £1m raised for the Cancer Trust a reality. He hit on a perfect means of spreading the message, creating an instant "thumbsupforstephen" campaign that encouraged people to share pictures of themselves raising their thumbs in the cancer patient's honour.

As the media around the world were swift to report, the pay-off was record-breaking in its speed and scale for the fundraising site JustGiving.com. Incredibly almost £5m was raised and people are still donating.

The comedian explained to the media why he was inspired to act after he had looked at Stephen's website and saw some of the stuff he had written. He thought that it was so intelligent and profound even though he had every right to be bitter and angry and he wasn't. It put things in perspective for him. Jason explained that he had spent the whole morning moaning because he couldn't find his children's shoes and then he couldn't find a parking space. He got stuck in traffic, got a flat tyre and had to spend an hour getting it changed. Then he read what Stephen had written and thought "None of these problems matter." He was inspired to do something positive to help Stephen in his fund raising efforts.

Performing random acts of kindness can be simple. It could be something like spending some time with an elderly person who lives alone. You could give up your seat on a bus or train, volunteer to help a project or charity in your local community or donate some unwanted possessions to a worthy cause. An act of kindness can be the foundation for great change in the world and be a contribution to making it a better place.

**Reflection time**

Pause for a few moments and reflect on the following question:

How can you make a difference to the life of others this week by performing random acts of kindness?

## 42. Live now – procrastinate later!

> "The best way to get something done is to begin."
> **Author unknown.**

One of the most common reasons that some people don't fulfil their potential or accomplish their personal ambitions is because they procrastinate and put things off.

Quite often, people have clarity on what they would like to achieve or want to do, they know the decision they need to make, they accept and understand the conversation that needs to be had or the path that they need to follow. They know in their hearts or their intuition tells them what action steps they need to take. Despite this clarity, many people still avoid taking action, they distract themselves and procrastinate.

Many people find it difficult to make decisions that will result in significant change to their and other people's lives. As a result of delaying making choices they may miss valuable opportunities to change things for the better. Delay in decision making and taking responsibility for changing things, may also result in them losing control of some issues and situations. It can mean they go on accepting unsatisfactory situations. This causes unnecessary anxiety and worry for themselves and those closest to them.

Some of the reasons for procrastination that I have come across include a fear of taking the wrong decision and suffering failure; dwelling on past bad experiences and mistakes and being uncertain about the future and the outcome of actions; feeling overwhelmed and believing that a task is too big and complex.

Understanding why people procrastinate is simple; figuring out how to overcome it isn't always easy. Conquering procrastination is near the top of many people's list of priorities for self-development. Minimising the effect of procrastination helps people to lead a productive, efficient and happy life. Some suggestions to overcome procrastination are detailed below:

- Get into the habit of taking action on your toughest task first each day – this helps to build momentum.
- If necessary, tackle large or complex tasks in small pieces – break them down into manageable chunks.
- Give up a need for perfectionism – aim for excellence rather than perfection.
- Commit yourself to action – set a deadline and start taking action. Tell others of your intended finish date - we don't like to lose face, so it will act as an added motivator to get the task completed.
- Make a definite commitment to overcome indecision and increase your willingness to make quicker decisions over the next year. There's no need to invest more time and energy on making a decision than is necessary.
- When faced with a decision, get clear on the outcome you would like to achieve. What would constitute an ideal outcome? What are the time frames?
- Get a clear definition of purpose for following a particular course. Write it down and articulate your motivations for wanting to effect the change or achieve the goal.
- Gather all the necessary facts, consider your options, and consider the best/worst case scenarios. List the pros and cons of the possible courses of action, evaluate the opportunities and risks.

- Choose your best option and decide to act.
- Plan your action steps, set some deadlines and get into action.

As I mentioned earlier, sometimes we feel overwhelmed by a task and it prevents us from taking action. An example may be cleaning out your loft or garage space. You have boxes and stuff everywhere and just the thought of the task seems daunting and stops you taking action. A way to overcome this is to set aside 20 minutes a day to sort through one or two boxes. This makes the task more manageable and builds momentum.

Get into the habit of setting and honouring deadlines. It's easy to feel alone with your challenges, but when it comes to overcoming procrastination there are probably many people in your network that can help you. Maybe you have a friend or relative that has a problem with procrastination. Perhaps you can encourage and hold each other to account.

**Reflection time:**

Pause for a few moments and reflect on the following questions:

Is there something you have been putting off that needs to be dealt with? What's the first step you can take to get started?

### 43. You are never too old to pursue a dream

> "You are never too old to set another goal or to dream a new dream." C. S. Lewis.

In November 2015 I enjoyed watching Jeff Lynne's Electric Light Orchestra perform in concert for BBC Radio 2. ELO enjoyed tremendous success across the world in the 1970's and 1980's producing great tracks like Mr Blue Sky, Livin' Thing and Don't Bring Me Down.

Prior to the show, I heard Jeff Lynne (now 68) interviewed and he explained that he thought his days of delivering concerts were over in 1985. Since then he has established himself as a very successful record producer.

However, in 2014 he was persuaded to be part of the Radio 2 live concert in Hyde Park. He stated that he was extremely nervous prior to going on stage given he hadn't played a concert for almost 30 years. He thought that it wouldn't be a very big audience and that not many people would be interested in watching their set because they were only interested in watching the headline acts perform later. Therefore he was amazed and thrilled to play to 50,000 people who seemed to really enjoy the show!

This positive experience inspired him to go back to his home in Los Angeles and write some new material and record a new album which was released in November 2015. They also arranged a tour of various arenas and they will be playing to sell out audiences!

It's always wonderful to see people start a new chapter in their life and enjoy a renaissance in their later years. The advances in medicine mean that people are living longer. Therefore it's possible to experience and do things in our old age that wouldn't have seemed to be possible 40 or 50 years ago. There are many possibilities for people to explore.

It made me think of all the times that I've heard people talk about a dream they had when they were younger or talk with a touch of regret about something that they've always wanted or would like to do but haven't yet accomplished. Only to say "but I am too old now."

A story that I love which counters this limiting belief, is the story of Cliff Young, an Australian potato farmer and athlete, best known for his unexpected win of the Sydney to Melbourne ultra-marathon (543 miles) in 1983 at 61 years of age.

What makes this feat even more incredible is the way that Cliff went about winning the race. It's normally only attempted by world class athletes, who train specially for the event and are typically less than 30 years of age. In fact it was the first race that Cliff had entered!

When he showed up at the start of the race in 1983, Cliff was wearing overalls and work boots! Everyone watching was shocked to discover Cliff wasn't a spectator when he picked up his race number and joined the other runners.

He was told that he was crazy and there was no way he would finish the race. To which he replied "Yes I can. See, I grew up on a farm where we couldn't afford horses or tractors, and the whole time I was growing up, whenever the storms would roll in, I'd have to go out and round up the sheep. We had 2,000 sheep on 2,000 acres. Sometimes I would have to run those sheep for two or three days. It took a long time, but I'd always catch them. I believe I can run this race."

Once the race was underway, Cliff didn't even run properly; he appeared to shuffle. Many people feared for the farmer's safety. The professional athletes knew that it took about 5 days to finish the race. In order to compete, they ran about 18 hours a day and slept for the remaining 6 hours.

Cliff wasn't constrained by conventional wisdom. He was unaware of this approach to the race. Whilst the top athletes slept, he kept on running! To everybody's disbelief, Cliff ran the whole five days without any sleep and secured an amazing victory!

Today, the "Young-shuffle" has been adopted by ultra-marathon runners because it is considered more energy-efficient.

**Reflection time:**

Pause for a few moments and reflect on the following questions:

Is there something that you dream of doing but haven't yet accomplished?

Are you able to take some action to make it happen?

What could be your first step?

## 44. A different perspective on time management

> "We cannot change the cards that we are dealt just how we play the hand." Randy Pausch.

Randy Pausch was an American University professor who learned that he had pancreatic cancer in September 2006 and in August 2007 he was given a terminal diagnosis: "3 to 6 months of good health left." He gave an upbeat lecture titled "The Last Lecture: Really Achieving Your Childhood Dreams" on September 18, 2007 and then co-authored a book called The Last Lecture. Here is what Randy had to say on the topic.

"All my life, I've been very aware that time is finite. I admit that I'm overly logical about a lot of things, but I firmly believe that one of my most appropriate fixations has been to manage time well. I've railed about time management to my students. I've given lectures on it. And because I've gotten good at it, I really do feel I was able to pack a whole lot of life into the shortened lifespan that I have been handed. Here's what I know:

**Ask yourself: Are you spending your time on the right things?**

You may have causes, goals, interests. Are they even worth pursuing? I've a clipping from a newspaper in Roanoke, Virginia. It featured a photo of a pregnant woman who'd lodged a protest against a local construction site. She worried that the sound of jackhammers was injuring her unborn child. But get this, in the photo; the woman is holding a cigarette. If she cared about her unborn child, the time she spent railing against jackhammers would have been better spent putting out that cigarette.

**Develop a good filing system**

When I told my wife I wanted to have a place in the house where we could file everything in alphabetical order, she said I sounded way too compulsive for her tastes. I told her that filing in alphabetical order is better than running around and saying I know it was blue and I know I was eating something when I had it!

**You can always change your plan but only if you have one**

I'm a big believer in to do lists. It helps us to break life into small steps. I once put "get tenure" on my to do list. That was naive. The most useful to do lists breaks tasks into small steps, like when I get my son to clean his room by picking up one thing at a time.

**Rethink the telephone**

I live in a culture where I spend lots of time on hold, listening to "your call is very important to us." I make sure that I am never on hold with a phone against my ear. I always use a speaker phone, so my hands are free to do something else.

**Delegate**

I learned early on that I could trust bright, nineteen year old students with the keys to my kingdom. It's never too early to delegate. My daughter Chloe is just eighteen months old, but two of my favourite photos are of her in my arms. In the first, I'm giving her a bottle. In the second, I've delegated the task to her. She looks satisfied. Me too.

**Take time out**

It's not a real vacation if you are reading emails or calling in for messages. When my wife and I went on our honeymoon, we wanted to be left alone. My boss, however, felt that I needed to provide a way for people to contact me. So I came up with the perfect phone message:

"Hi, this is Randy. I waited until I was thirty-nine to get married, so my wife and I are going away for a month. I hope you don't have a problem with that, but my boss does. Apparently, I have to be reachable." I then gave the names of my wife's parents and the city where they live. I told them that if they call directory assistance that they could get their number and if they convince my new in-laws that their emergency merits interrupting their only daughter's honeymoon, they have our number. We didn't get any calls!

Some of my time management tips are dead on serious and some are a bit tongue in cheek. But I believe all of them are worth considering. Time is all you have and one day you may find that you have less than you think."

**Reflection time:-**

Pause for a few moments and reflect on the following question:

What steps can you take to improve the way that you manage time?

## 45. Are you having fun at work?

**"Choose a job you love, and you will never have to work a day in your life." Confucius.**

Genius is a term that is too easily used these days but in Terry Wogan's case it was appropriate. He was a broadcasting genius, who for over 50 years brought much pleasure to many people. His BBC Radio 2 breakfast show pulled in over 8 million listeners and he was popular across many different age groups.

He seemed to really enjoy his work and went about it with a smile on his face and a great sense of humour. His approach was infectious and spread lots of happiness. He didn't seem to take himself too seriously and made his radio shows about the listener. When asked how many listeners he had, he replied "just one." He was relaxed, natural and made what he was doing look effortless and easy. As a result he put people at ease and was a great role model for ensuring that you enjoy your work.

A story that captured the essence of his personality involves when he met Her Majesty the Queen. Apparently, the Queen asked him how long he had worked at the BBC. With his customary charm and wit he replied that he had never done a day's work at the BBC! Essentially he just loved what he did and didn't consider it to be work! What a wonderful aspiration for all of us to really enjoy the work we do.

A few days after Terry died, I was on a train and I reflected on his career and comments to the Queen. I glanced around the crowded quiet carriage at the various commuters and wondered how many of them were truly happy with their job.

We spend so much of our life working; I believe it's vital we enjoy what we do. There is a universal truth that covers us all. Whether you are Richard Branson, one of his airline's pilots, cabin or ground crew, you have the same amount of time available to you each week:- 24 hours a day, 7 days a week, 168 hours in total.

I know of many people who regularly spend over 50 hours a week at work, preparing for and travelling to and from work and working at home in the evenings/weekends. That amounts to almost one third of their available time, add in 50 odd hours for sleep and that leaves just 68 hours for everything else.

I always stress to business owners and leaders about the importance of encouraging their people to have some fun during the working day and the benefits they will attain from this philosophy. I strongly believe that we do best what we enjoy and feel passionate about.

Fun at work also helps to increase creativity and productivity. Research published in 2014, led by Professor Andrew Oswald, Dr Eugenio Proto and Dr Daniel Sgroi from the Department of Economics, University of Warwick claimed that happiness at work led to a 12% increase in productivity, while unhappy workers proved 10% less productive. As the research team put it, "We find that human happiness has large and positive causal effects on productivity. Positive emotions appear to invigorate human beings."

During the experiments a number of the participants were either shown a comedy movie clip or treated to free chocolate, drinks and fruit. Others were questioned about recent family tragedies, such as bereavements, to assess whether lower levels of happiness were later associated with lower levels of productivity.

Professor Oswald said: "Companies like Google have invested more in employee support and employee satisfaction has risen as a result. For Google, it rose by 37%; they know what they are talking about. Under scientifically controlled conditions, making workers happier really pays off."

Dr Sgroi added: "The driving force seems to be that happier workers use the time they have more effectively, increasing the pace at which they can work without sacrificing quality."

Shawn Anchor, author of The Happiness Advantage suggests that people who cultivate a positive mindset perform better and every business outcome shows improvement. Anchor also states that individuals tend to be more creative, better at solving problems and they're more effective collaborators working toward common goals when they are happy and positive. As Anchor sees it, the incentive for organisations is clear-cut — "happiness leads to greater levels of profits" for companies that take the right steps.

**Reflection time:**

Pause for a few moments and reflect on the following question:

What steps can you take to increase the amount of fun you have?

## 46. Developing patience

> "Patience and perseverance have a magical effect before which difficulties disappear and obstacles vanish."
> **John Quincy Adams.**

A client who was settling into a new leadership position, asked me to help develop her leadership effectiveness and influencing skills. During one of the sessions, she said that she wanted to cultivate greater patience as she was concerned that her current approach to life wasn't sustainable or particularly enjoyable.

She had always been a high achiever, very focused, hardworking and determined. She achieved the objectives she set for herself or had been asked to deliver by others. However, the results came at a cost. She took too much responsibility for projects, not delegating sufficiently because she didn't feel she had enough time to explain to her staff what she wanted or seek their input. This meant she didn't help them develop and conceded that she wasn't getting the best out of them.

She found it difficult to switch off when not at work, her sleep pattern was erratic and this combination had a negative impact on her home life and close relationships. She told me that she felt pressured, irritated and frustrated if things didn't move as quickly as she would like. She had a constant feeling inside of anxiety, was very self-critical and hard on herself. She explained she was more impatient and intolerant with herself than with others. She confessed that she was afraid to change and ease up as she was frightened that she wouldn't be able to deliver the results that she had become accustomed to.

We discussed the definition of patience, which the dictionary defines as "the capacity to accept or tolerate delay, problems, or suffering without becoming annoyed or anxious."

I explained to her that it was always advisable when embarking on this kind of major behavioural change to get clear on the benefits the new approach will bring. This means that when the going gets tough and you consider reverting back to your old habits, you can remind yourself why you are seeking to change. This provides the energy and determination to persist with your new approach.

She said that the benefits for her would be that she would feel less anxious, enjoy better relationships and engagement with others, her staff would develop, her sleep would improve and life would be generally more enjoyable. She stated that her motivation for changing was that she wanted a more sustainable approach to her work and life, less stress, which would improve her health and probably the length of her life.

The client made the necessary changes and is still generating great results. She is more relaxed, happy and enjoying her downtime from work. Her relationships have improved and she is delegating more and as a result her staff are growing and developing.

Here are some tips on developing patience, which really helped the client I have referred to and I hope they help you too:-

- Clarify the differences between the things that you can control and influence and the things that you can't. Spend the bulk of your time on the things you can control. Let go of things over which you have no control or influence.

- Get clarity on the big goals that you want to achieve. Take time to re-evaluate your personal priorities and what's important to you. Get clear on the goals that really matter from this moment on. As you know, goals are best achieved by breaking them into small chunks.
- Introduce the word acceptance into your vocabulary. Accept people don't always move at your pace. Accept them for what they are not how you want them to be. Accept that things don't always go as you would like. Learn to work with how things are today right now, rather than wasting time, energy and thought wishing that things were different.
- Display prominent reminders of your new approach. Create an affirmation such as "I am in the process of developing greater patience, making the most of each day and living in the present." Place it on your bathroom mirror, on your phone, tablet, pc or car dashboard.
- Learn to forgive yourself. Accept that you are human, will occasionally make mistakes or that things will not work out as you imagined. If you make a mistake, accept it, learn from it and move on.

**Reflection time:**

Pause for a few moments and reflect on the following question:

If you developed greater patience what benefits would it bring you?

## 47. What stops you asking for what you want?

### "Ask for what you want and be prepared to get it."
### Maya Angelou.

I really enjoyed watching a film called Marvellous, a true story of a life lived to the full, about a man once labelled with 'learning difficulties' whose life defies limitations. I thoroughly recommend that you watch the film if you get the opportunity.

It tells the beautiful, funny, true story of Neil Baldwin, who has been a circus clown; a lay preacher; kit man at Stoke City football club (former team manager Lou Macari has often described him as his best-ever signing).

He's on first name terms with leading sportsmen and senior clergy. He was awarded an Honorary Degree by Keele University for the contributions he has made to campus life there across the last 50 years.

There were many simple pieces of wisdom throughout the programme which we can all learn from. For instance, someone asked Neil how he stayed so positive. He said that he always wanted to be happy, so he decided to be! He said that if bad things happen, he just thought about the good things. He remarked that none of us are getting any younger but that's life and we have to make the most of it.

In one scene he's talking to his friend about how each year he watched the annual university boat race on the River Thames from the umpire's boat. His friend asked him how he managed to get a place on the boat. Neil's answer was simple; he said "I asked." The friend said "you can't do that by asking." Neil paused and said "I can."

This scene got me thinking about what stops us all asking for help or what we want. I wondered what we miss out on when we don't ask. I've found that people don't ask for what they want because they don't want to impose on people, look needy or weak. Another major reason is that they afraid of being rejected and hearing the word no.

Many years ago, I participated in a training event attended by several hundred people. As part of the workshop within a designated timeframe, we had to talk to as many of the participants as possible about something we were passionate about and seek their help. We also had to listen to other peoples stories and consider their requests for help.

One of the rules of the exercise was that we had to say no to nine people and were only allowed to say yes to the tenth person we spoke to. It didn't matter how moving the story was or how persuasive or passionate the person was, we could only say yes on one out of ten occasions.

It was a really interesting exercise, you learned that the more you ask, the more likely you are to get a yes. It helped you to get used to handling rejection. Additionally it taught you that although you got a no, it wasn't because your story wasn't compelling or people didn't believe in it. It just wasn't the right time and they weren't in a position to help at that moment. If you approached them at a later time they may be able to say yes. It proved the importance of persistence and follow up.

Another big realisation for lots of the participants was how good they felt when they were able to say yes and help people.

**Here are a few tips in getting better at asking for what you want:**

- If you don't ask the answer is already no! The more you ask the more likely you are to get a yes
- Be clear and specific about what it is that you want or need help with
- If you get a no, don't take it personally. It's not rejection; it's just that your request didn't resonate with the person at that time
- Be confident in the way that you ask for help. Talk from the heart and with passion but guard against being too pushy and making people feel uncomfortable. Observe and respond to the person's body language.
- When you get a "no" tell yourself that you are one step closer to getting a yes
- Follow up. If you got a no, it's not a no forever, keep in touch and you may get a yes in the future. When you ask for help and get a yes, say thank you and keep the person informed on how things are going.

**Reflection time:**

Pause for a few moments and reflect on the following questions:

How good are you at asking for what you want?

Is there something you need to ask for at the moment?

## 48. Keep things simple – less is more sometimes

*"Success is nothing more than a few simple disciplines, practiced every day."* Jim Rohn.

Life is busy and the world is changing at a faster rate than any time in history. The advancement and development of technology has increased the speed of communication and raised expectations about response times. It has also given us access to a wealth of information and ways to entertain ourselves.

The pace of change is phenomenal. According to some research detailed in a book called Sort Your Brain Out by Dr Jack Lewis and Adrian Webster, in 1984 there were just 1000 devices hooked up to the internet across the globe. Eight years later in 1992, the number hit the one million mark. The one billion mark was crossed in 2008. There were 4 Exabytes of new data created in 2012, that's 4 billion billion bytes; more information in a single year than in the 5000 preceding years put together.

The scale of change is touching every facet of our lives. How we work and communicate with each other, stay in touch with family, friends and business contacts. It influences the way we shop, gather information and learn. It impacts us in so many different ways. Many years ago a trip to Australia from the UK would have taken weeks by boat. Now it takes seconds to connect to someone on the other side of the world via video conferencing.

Increasingly, I'm seeing more examples of people feeling overwhelmed and juggling many different priorities, whilst still seeking to sustain high levels of performance and have a balanced happy life. Technology is amazing however, it brings challenges. It's said that the conscious brain can only handle 7 bits of information at any one time and that's a main reason why we can feel overloaded and distracted. It can mean we lose focus, sight of our key priorities and what really matters to us.

I was talking with a client who was contemplating leaving their successful corporate career and making a transition into self-employment. They felt that it was the right time in their life to pause, re-evaluate, and redefine happiness and how they measure success. They told me that they wanted greater time to enjoy the simple things in life, have more quality time with their family and experience increased richness in life with less.

During our conversation, the following story about a Mexican Fisherman came to mind and I shared it with my client.

An American businessman was at the pier of a small coastal Mexican fishing village when a small boat with just one fisherman docked. Inside the boat were several large yellow-fin tuna. The American complimented the Mexican on the quality of his fish and asked how long it took to catch them.

The Mexican replied, "Only a little while, senor." The American asked why he didn't stay out longer and catch more fish. The Mexican said that he had enough to supply his family's immediate needs.

The American then asked, "But what do you do with the rest of your time?"

The fisherman said, "I play with my children, take a siesta with my wife Maria, stroll into the village each evening where I sip wine and play the guitar with my amigos. I have a full and busy life, senor."

The American smiled, "I have a Harvard MBA, that's a degree in business studies, I could help you. You should spend more time fishing and with the proceeds buy a bigger boat, with the income from the bigger boat you could buy several boats, eventually you would have a fleet. Then instead of selling your catch to a middleman you would sell directly to the processor, eventually opening your own cannery. You would control the product, processing and distribution. You would, of course, need to leave this small coastal fishing village and move to Mexico City, then Los Angeles and eventually New York City where you would run your expanding enterprise."

The Mexican fisherman asked, "But, senor, how long would all this take?" The American replied, "Fifteen to twenty years." "But what then, senor?"

The American laughed, "That's the best part. When the time is right you sell your stock to the public and become very rich. You would make millions." "Millions, senor? But then what?"

"Then you would retire, move to a small coasting fishing village, where you could sleep late, fish a little, play with your kids, take a siesta with your wife Maria, and stroll to the village in the evenings where you could sip wine and play your guitar with your amigos."

With just the hint of a twinkle in his eye, the fisherman said, "Senor – are these business degrees hard to get?"

**Reflection time:**

Pause for a few moments and reflect on the following question:

What steps could you take to bring greater balance to your life?

## 49. Turning a personal vision into reality

**"A dream doesn't become reality through magic; it takes sweat, determination and hard work." Colin Powell.**

During a visit to Cornwall I managed to squeeze in a visit to the Minack Theatre and watch a production. The Minack is an open-air theatre, constructed above a gully with a rocky granite outcrop jutting into the sea. It's situated at Porthcurno which is 4 miles from Land's End. It has inspiring and breath-taking views over the neighbouring coast line. If you're lucky and it's a clear night, a sunset provides a fabulous bonus to the production.

Many visitors who arrive at the Minack imagine that it was built by invading Romans but the truth is the theatre was the brainchild of Rowena Cade. Miss Cade had moved to Cornwall after the First World War and built a house for herself and her mother on land at Minack Point for £100.

The history of the theatre as stated on the theatre website is that in 1929, a local village group of players had staged Shakespeare's A Midsummer Night's Dream in a nearby meadow at Crean, repeating the production the next year. They decided that their next production would be The Tempest. While Rowena Cade did think of offering her garden to stage "The Tempest" there really was nowhere to seat an audience.

Always resourceful she prospected alternatives, one of which was on the opposite side of the bay. Then, looking into the gully above the Minack rock she said "I wonder if we could make a stage here?" With the benefit of decades of hindsight and with her remarkable theatre spread out below, the answer was clearly "Yes!"

Over the course of six months and during a harsh winter, Miss Cade and her gardener, Billy Rawlings, made a terrace and rough seating, hauling materials down from the house or up via the winding path from the beach below. In 1932, The Tempest was performed with the sea as a dramatic backdrop, to great success. Miss Cade resolved to improve the theatre, working over the course of the winter months each year throughout her life (with the help of Billy Rawlings and Charles Angove) so that others might perform each summer.

Over the next seven years there were many improvements and extensions. Then, with the coming of World War II, it seemed as though all the back-breaking work might have been wasted. When peace returned, Rowena looked out over a ravaged theatre. It had been reduced back to what it had been in 1932. However, with great determination Rowena slowly brought the Minack magic back to life, working on improving and developing the theatre for over 50 years.

Looking at pictures now, it's remarkable what she and her two helpers achieved. Apparently she worked each winter in all weathers until she was in her mid-eighties. When she died, just short of her ninetieth birthday, she was still thinking of the future. She left elaborate sketches suggesting how the Theatre might be covered on the days when it rains.

This frail looking lady must have had tremendous strength and determination to achieve her vision. It's quite remarkable what she managed to create and leave as a legacy. It's a facility that has thousands of visitors each year and brings pleasure to many who are grateful for Rowena's work and perseverance. After visiting the theatre, a few things occurred to me about the power of having a personal vision and goal setting in general. I have shared these thoughts below:-

- When you set a goal or have a personal vision, you have no comprehension of the potential impact it can have on hundreds of thousands of people and the positive ripple it can create.
- It's incredible what a few committed individuals with a common purpose (working without machinery) can achieve. Truly remarkable and inspiring.
- When you have a vision it require lots of determination and perseverance to help you overcome obstacles and set-backs that you encounter along the way.
- Your commitment and resolve will be tested but when you meet and conquer the adversity you emerge stronger and wiser for the experience. You can then look back with a sense of pride at your accomplishment.
- It's possible to create something that outlasts you.

**Reflection time:**

Pause for a few moments and reflect on the following questions:

Is there a goal that you have that you haven't taken action on recently? What one step would re-ignite and re-energise this goal?

## 50. What's the worst thing that can happen?

*"Always do what you are afraid to do."*
**Ralph Waldo Emerson.**

The company that a client worked for was going through a merger and understandably he was feeling a little anxious and stressed about the potential changes. He had a mortgage and family to support and was wondering what he would do for a job if he were made redundant. He was also concerned about the financial implications.

The client is extremely talented, good at his job and well respected by his colleagues. He has been with the company for almost 10 years and one of their top performers. I believed he was someone the organisation would want to retain.

I asked him if he'd been given the impression that he was unlikely to secure a position with the reshaped company. He said that wasn't the case as he'd been told they were looking to ensure there was a position. However, he thought that it may be a different role with changed responsibilities. I asked why he was feeling so anxious and uncertain if it looked like he'd still have a job once the merger was completed.

He explained that part of him was wondering if he could view it as an opportunity to do something different. He said that he would really like to start his own business and have a fresh challenge. However, he wasn't sure that he had the necessary courage to make this move. Having worked for the same company for so long he wasn't certain he was equipped to work for himself. I explained this was a common thought pattern.

He conceded that he was scared of the unknown and stepping outside his comfort zone. However there was another part of him that was excited at the prospect of being his own boss and master of his destiny. He was certainly being pulled in different directions.

Many people adopt a similar stance about their potential and capability when faced with similar circumstances to what is described above. Most people don't realise what treasure lies within them. As I've said previously sometimes the biggest limits that we have are the ones in our own minds.

I mentioned to my client the story about the way that baby elephants are trained. Control is established while the elephant is very small. A chain is placed around the baby elephant's leg and attached to a three foot iron stake which is driven into the ground. Therefore for several days the baby elephant pulls and tugs and strains against the stake and the chain. However, he is too small to dislodge it.

Soon he's convinced by this experience that the three foot stake and chain have the power to bind him. He no longer attempts to pull free. Years later, when the elephant is fully grown, weighing thousands of pounds and capable of uprooting trees or pulling a car, he can still be held by a three foot stake! Yet, if that stake were as big and planted as deep as a telephone pole, he could easily uproot it! How does the stake and chain hold the elephant? The answer is control and conditioning.

Sometimes I think our lives reflect the story of the elephant. We get so conditioned to a certain way of life and thinking that we believe that we aren't capable of doing anything new.

Whilst we may have a desire to test ourselves, which may include starting our own venture, it's never an easy decision to give up on what's known and relatively safe. You have to overcome the inner voice that tells you that you're crazy to contemplate such a move.

I suggested to my client that he needed to evaluate the pros and cons attached to the potential change and get comfortable with the risks attached. I suggested that he ask himself a question which I suggest to all people who are contemplating major change and transition in their lives. The question is "What is the worst thing that can happen?"

I explained he needed to be completely honest with himself and ensure that he was at ease with the worst case scenario(s) that this question unearthed. If after this process he felt he was equipped to step into the unknown he could decide his next steps. Getting comfortable with the worst thing that could happen, would give him the confidence and courage to take the leap of faith. He went for it and hasn't looked back.

**Reflection time:**

Pause for a few moments and reflect on the following question:

What changes would you make to your life if you knew that you couldn't fail?

## 51. We are powerful beyond measure

**"I learned that courage was not the absence of fear, but the triumph over it. The brave man is not he who does not feel afraid, but he who conquers that fear." Nelson Mandela.**

When I ask workshop delegates to name a person who has inspired them, a popular choice is Nelson Mandela. They explain they are impressed by the way he fought for justice and freedom, overcame adversity and showed forgiveness. He allowed many people to believe in the creation of a better world.

Here are some insights and lessons we can draw from some of Nelson Mandela's quotations:-

### Be committed to your beliefs

"I have cherished the ideal of a democratic and free society in which all persons live together in harmony and with equal opportunities. It's an ideal which I hope to live for and to achieve. But if needs be, it's an ideal for which I am prepared to die."

He spent 27 years in prison for fighting against apartheid government in South Africa.

### The world is a better place when we work together

"A fundamental concern for others in our individual and community lives would go a long way in making the world the better place we so passionately dreamt of."

Regardless of age, sex, creed or colour, we've all been put in this world together.

### The things worth having in life are the hardest to come by

"Difficulties break some men but make others. No axe is sharp enough to cut the soul of a sinner who keeps on trying, one armed with the hope that he will rise even in the end."

The people that persevere and push through their challenges accomplish goals.

### Knowledge is power

"Education is the most powerful weapon which you can use to change the world."

Education and knowledge equips you to develop and manage change.

### We are responsible for our life and choices

"I am the master of my fate and the captain of my destiny."

You have to take control of the steering wheel of your life, your results and progress is down to you.

### Be optimistic

"I'm fundamentally an optimist. Whether that comes from nature or nurture, I cannot say. Part of being optimistic is keeping one's head pointed toward the sun, one's feet moving forward. There were many dark moments when my faith in humanity was sorely tested, but I wouldn't and couldn't give myself up to despair. That way lays defeat and death."

Looking at the glass as half full helps you to stay positive and energised.

**Make a difference to others**

"What counts in life is not the mere fact that we have lived. It's what difference we have made to the lives of others that will determine the significance of the life we lead."

It makes the world a better and more meaningful place if we look to make a positive difference to the life of others.

**One can overcome poverty**

"Overcoming poverty is not a task of charity; it is an act of justice. Like slavery and apartheid, poverty is not natural. It is man-made and it can be overcome and eradicated by the actions of human beings. Sometimes it falls on a generation to be great. You can be that great generation. Let your greatness blossom."

This quote sums up his belief that people have the resources to enable them to flourish.

When Nelson Mandela became South Africa's president, he used the following passage from Marianne Williamson's Return to Love in his inaugural speech. I've always found it to be a great reminder of the opportunities and possibilities available in life. It encourages us to be expansive in our thinking and to shine our light brightly in the world.

"Our deepest fear is not that we are inadequate. Our deepest fear is that we are powerful beyond measure.

It is our light not our darkness that most frightens us. We ask ourselves, "Who am I to be brilliant, gorgeous, talented, and fabulous?"

Actually, who are you not to be?

You are a child of God. You're playing small does not serve the world; there is nothing enlightening about shrinking so that other people won't feel insecure around us.

We are meant to shine, as children do. We are born to manifest the glory of God that is within us.

It is not just in some of us, it's in everyone and as we let our light shine we unconsciously give other people permission to do the same.

As we are liberated from our fear our presence automatically liberates others."

**Reflection time:-**

Pause for a few moments and reflect on the following question:

How can you shine your light more brightly in the world?

## 52. 16 Tips to help you to Be First Class professionally and personally

> *"Great things are done by a series of small things brought together."* Vincent Van Gogh.

So we've arrived at chapter 52 and the conclusion of the book. As I'm finishing writing this book in 2016, I thought that it was appropriate for the final chapter to include a summary of 16 ideas and best practices to help you to Be First Class personally and professionally. They are some of the key messages contained in the book. I hope that you find them helpful.

### 1. Have a clear vision and goals for the year

Be clear about what you would like to experience and achieve this year. As well as professional goals, ensure you have at least 3-5 main personal goals for the year ahead.

### 2. Quit comparing yourself to others

This will save a lot of mental energy and focus. We are all unique and have different life experiences, so instead of comparing your results to others, compare them to the targets you set.

### 3. Spend more time in the present moment

You can't change what has happened and the future is a mystery. Quit worrying about the past and living life too far in the future. Don't let yesterday or tomorrow take up too much of today.

4. **Let go of the things you can't control**

It's easy to spend your time thinking and worrying about things outside your control. Instead focus your time and energy on things that you can control and positively influence.

5. **Develop an attitude of gratitude**

Each day take time to really appreciate all that you have in your life. Make a note of at least 3 things daily in a notebook. Celebrate your successes, achievements and good fortune.

6. **Prioritise self- care**

Good health is the real wealth in life, so focus on your health and well-being. A daily brisk walk is a good way to do 30 minutes exercise. Have a break at lunch time and quit eating at your desk.

7. **Listen to and trust your intuition**

Get into the habit of tuning in, listening and trusting your intuition. It knows what's best for you. If it says go for it, listen to that wisdom. If it doesn't feel right heed the warning.

8. **Be impeccable with your word**

Say only what you mean. Keep the promises that you make to yourself and others. Promise only what you intend and can fulfil. Speak with integrity and avoid negative language, gossip and bad mouthing others.

## 9. Tame the e mail monster

Check them no more than twice a day. Unsubscribe from some lists. Encourage colleagues to mail only what's essential. Advocate an internal e mail free day each week in your business.

## 10. Have a technology free day each week

Give your brain a break and switch off your phone, computers and avoid social media. Be really present with activities and conversations with family and friends or spend time outdoors.

## 11. Develop your positivity muscle

Create a positivity book to record positive experiences, feedback and good fortune. What you focus on and nurture grows. Be an example to others and be the most positive person you know.

## 12. Be yourself – everyone else is taken!

Stand up for what you believe in. Be true to yourself and your values. You are unique and special and in a world where you can be anything, it's important to be yourself.

## 13. Practice random acts of kindness

Doing unexpected and unconditional good deeds for others create good feelings. It can be a simple gesture and doesn't have to cost money. It helps to create a better world.

### 14. Make room for fun and laughter

There is much research available to endorse the health benefits of frequent laughter. Make time to watch funny movies or TV shows or read a funny book. See the funny side of life often.

### 15. Ask for help when you need it

You can't do it all alone. Seek out help for your areas of limitation and gaps in your knowledge and resources. See it as strength to ask for help when you need it rather than a weakness.

### 16. Live now – procrastinate later.

Quit over thinking and get into action. Regularly ask yourself "what would I do today if I were brave?" Follow up on your ideas and action plans. The fortune is always in the follow up!

**Reflection time:**

Pause for a few moments and reflect on the following question:

Which of the tips do you need to focus more attention on to help you to be the best you can be?

**Promise yourself** - Christian D Larson

To be so strong that nothing can disturb your peace of mind.
To talk health, happiness, and prosperity to every person you meet.

To make all your friends feel that there is something worthwhile in them.
To look at the sunny side of everything and make your optimism come true.

To think only the best, to work only for the best and to expect only the best.
To be just as enthusiastic about the success of others as you are about your own.

To forget the mistakes of the past and press onto the greater achievements of the future.
To wear a cheerful countenance at all times and give every living creature you meet a smile.

To give so much time to the improvement of yourself that you have no time to criticise others.
To be too large for worry, too noble for anger, too strong for fear and too happy to permit the presence of trouble.

To think well of yourself and to proclaim this fact to the world, not in loud words but great deeds.
To live in faith that the whole world is on your side so long as you are true to the best that is in you.

**About the author**

Stephen Pauley has worked as an executive coach and facilitator since 2001, following a successful 18 year corporate career where he gained valuable leadership, sales and customer service experience. This practical knowledge is the foundation of his work.

Stephen helps clients grow results and develop their leadership skills to increase engagement and accountability in their teams. He supports clients to gain clarity on their main priorities and helps develop their presentation and communication skills so that they communicate clearly and with impact.

He has worked with thousands of individuals and teams nationally (in the UK) and internationally and has experience of working in a variety of sectors including Accountancy, Agro-chemicals, Banking, Charities, Government Agencies, Hospitality, IT, Legal, Media, Retail, Oil and Gas, Pharmaceuticals, Telecoms and Universities. His clients range from leaders in blue chip companies, public sector organisations and small and medium sized enterprises through to start up entrepreneurs.

Stephen enjoys working with teams and facilitates energised, fun and participative team events which demonstrate how team performance can be transformed through greater collaboration, innovation and focus. These workshops help to build greater commercial awareness within the team. He has also delivered a number of talks to staff and association conferences covering a range of development topics. For more information please visit www.befirstclass.co.uk or email Stephen@befirstclass.co.uk.